Camp and Trail Methods

INTERESTING INFORMATION FOR ALL LOVERS OF NATURE. WHAT TO TAKE AND WHAT TO DO

BY E. KREPS,
Author of "Science of Trapping."

PUBLISHED BY
A. R. HARDING
COLUMBUS, OHIO

ISBN 0-936622-01-6

CONTENTS.

LIST OF ILLUSTRATIONS.

7

E. KREPS.

INTRODUCTION.

A LIFE in the open air calls for knowledge which a very large number of human beings, because of their environments, cannot gain, except when the same is imparted by some more fortunate one who has learned it from experience. There are many who live this out-door life and these old and seasoned woodsmen know, perhaps, all that is contained in this book, but there are others, a much larger number, who do not know the many things relating to outdoor life, which it is almost necessary that one should be well acquainted with when he makes his initial journey into the fastnesses of Mother Nature. My object in getting out this work is to enlighten these would-be outers, to give them the information which will start them on the right trail, knowledge which cannot be had from any other source.

There are many works on woodcraft, written by sportsmen, fishermen, and campers but only a few of these books were written by practical woodsmen and for people who want to belong to that class. Such books are intended for the big game hunter, or the fisherman who goes for a short stay into some easily accessible location, well equipped, and with a guide who does all of the work and looks after the comfort of those whom he has in charge. This book is a decided departure from that class, as it not only gives the information needed by the tourist and summer camper, but gives special attention to the needs of those practical ones whose calling, whatever it may be, leads them into the wilds and holds them there at all times of the year; the hunter, the fisherman, the trapper, the prospector, the surveyor; all these and many others will find much valuable information in this book.

E KREPS.

Camp and Trail Methods

Portaging a Canoe.

CAMP AND TRAIL METHODS

CHAPTER I.

PLEASURES AND PROFITS OF CAMPING.

HAT can be more pleasant, and I will say, more profitable, to the tired, overworked business man, who has spent months in a stuffy office in the heart of some city, than to go away for a few weeks' vacation and to camp somewhere in the solitude of the forest, on the bank of a babbling brook or the shore of a lake, with a few congenial companions, there to while away the days in fishing, hunting, photography or some other out-of-door pastime; breathing the fresh, pure air and living close to Mother Nature!

I venture to make the assertion that if anything is more pleasing it is just a little more of the same thing. Then too, there is a certain gain in these periodical outings. After a few weeks, or a month of this style of living, one can again return to the city feeling that he has a new lease of life. His general health is better, his muscles have become hardened and both himself and his friends are surprised at the change.

Not only to the business man, but to the many others who by one means or other make a living in the great out-of-doors, these trips into the "wilds" are not only a source of profit but of pleasure also. It is not only the profit that takes the trapper into the fastnesses of nature, for I venture to say that comparatively few of them would go for profit if there was no pleasure connected with such a life.

There are many reasons why one should go into the wilderness and the fact that he goes, or wishes to do so, is reason enough why he should know all that is possible about camping and living in comfort when he has only himself and his meagre efforts to depend on. He may be a lone prospector, searching the quartz veins for the precious yellow metal, removed a hundred miles from civilization. All day he searches diligently breaking off a sample here and there, or washing a pan of sand and gravel from the shore of a little mountain stream, with his home, a small sheet of canvas with a blanket in a pack near by. It is taken with him everywhere and when night comes on he pitches his shelter and cooks his evening meal. Surely this is the simple life, the primordial kind, almost equalling in simplicity that of the earliest, most primitive human beings. He, of all persons must know the elements of woodcraft; he must be able to traverse the trackless wilds, day after day, without losing his bearings, must know how to provide himself with food and clothing, also shelter, how to treat the most common ailments and many other things pertaining to woods life, which to the ordinary mortal are hidden knowledge. But for all of his hardships, the lone prospector enjoys life and it would be almost impossible for him to give up his calling and take up one which is less strenuous.

Then, there is the trapper collecting his revenue, a bunch of fine and valuable furs, from the forest and the stream. His lot is in many ways harder than that of the prospector for he also is usually alone and in addition, he can only follow his calling during the colder seasons of the year, whereas, the prospector works mostly during the milder weather of summer.

I can say from experience that there is a certain indescribable pleasure in the long tramps over the blazed trail. Some people claim that the out-of-door man does not appreciate the advantages of his position, but this is a mistake.

The life of the trapper and prospector is not always a "bed of roses" but there is a certain amount of pleasure in even the roughest experiences, and in after years, when thinking of the past, he remembers only the pleasant events.

For myself, I have had many experiences which at the time I considered decidedly unpleasant. I have gone for long periods without food, camped out in all kinds of disagreeable weather, made such long trips that I was almost completely exhausted and suffered much from cold and other privations, and yet I look back on that same life with pleasure,—not at all sorry for the experience.

On one occasion which comes to mind, I was prospecting, in company with a friend, and we were caught one evening in a cold drenching rain. We had but a sorry shelter, at the best, but we hastened to pitch our camp for the night. A worse place for a camp could scarcely have been found, and we had to pass the night practically without wood or shelter, for the wind shifted continually, driving the cold rain under our shelter and drenching us to the skin. If ever two poor mortals were glad to see the light of day, we were on that occasion; however, we suffered no ill after-effects, and the last time I met my companion he recalled this incident, and spoke of it as though it had been one of his pleasant experiences.

Ages ago man was a savage, and though he has been under the restraining influences of civilization for centuries, the spirit of the savage is still strong within, therefore, when he hears the "call of the wild" as one of the popular writers has so aptly expressed it, I would advise packing up the kit and hieing off to some secluded spot to spend a few weeks in close communion with Mother Nature. And now, I think a few words regarding the outfit will be appropriate.

CHAPTER II.

SELECTING A CAMP OUTFIT.

HEN selecting an outfit for use in the woods, many things must be considered, such as the locality, the climate, the season, the object of the expedition, means of transportation, etc.

For instance, if one is going on a big game hunt he has only his hunting and camp outfit and food to think of, but if one is going for an extended trip, such as a trapping expedition, he has not only to think of his immediate needs, but must also think of the future, of the change of weather, of the probability of sickness or accident, and many other things which the sportsman, going only for a short camping trip, does not need to think of. If one is going far back into the wilds he cannot take such an outfit as the ordinary camper would select, and the list must be weeded down until there is not one article that is not absolutely needed.

Also many of the articles recommended in works on this subject may be omitted, in fact,

I think it wise to mention some of the things which should not be taken as well as that which is really needed. I have myself followed guiding to some extent, and was many times amused at the outfit taken by some of my employers; the long list of camp furniture, the odd and almost worthless articles of wearing apparel, etc. Surely, when one is going on a camping trip he does not desire to live just as he would at home, for in my opinion much of the pleasure of camping is derived from taking things just as we find them, of sleeping on a bed of boughs rather than on a cot, sitting on an old log rather than on a folding camp chair, and of eating off of the ground rather than from a table, in fact I think that most of the pleasure is in the novelty of the thing. And to the practical woodsman, this camp furniture is an abomination. I give here a list of the articles which will be actually needed for a hunting trip in any of the northern sections. It will be understood that these trips are made in the fall of the year, and the time devoted to the trip not to exceed one month. The list is as follows:

2 gray woolen shirts.
2 suits woolen underclothing.
4 pairs heavy woolen socks.
1 pair oil tanned moccasins, preferably with soles.

1 pair camp slippers.

1 soft hat medium width brim.

1 belt.

1 wall tent, size depending on number of persons in party.

1 camp stove with telescopic pipe.

1 pair woolen blankets for each person.

1 camp axe, with file and stone for sharpening.

1 belt axe, gun and ammunition, hunting knife, pocket compass, and a few toilet articles for each person.

If party is not too large, one large frying pan with socket for handle, two heavy tin kettles (nesting), and a fair size tin pail for making tea or coffee are all the cooking utensils which are actually needed. For table ware, a drinking cup, plate, knife, fork, and spoon for each. The white enameled table ware is best. One small mirror and comb, two towels and a cake or two of toilet soap will answer for the party. As for the food, etc., I will speak of that later.

For a more extended trip, say a winter's trapping, a somewhat different outfit will be needed, or rather the same outfit with some additional articles.

Parties going into the wilds for a considerable length of time invariably use the log camp, therefore, when making up the outfit the tent would be omitted. More clothing would be needed, also traps, snowshoes, repair kit, etc.

When selecting an outfit, the means of transportation must be considered, and whether it is packed a long distance overland or taken by canoe or boat, the weight of each article must be considered especially for the overland trip. In other words, the lightest articles should be selected, so long as the lightness does not detract from their strength and usefulness.

On most of the southern rivers one can go long distances by boat or canoe, and it is the custom among the trappers to move frequently from place to place. In such cases the tent must be used, and the camping outfit would be practically the same as listed. Of course, on such trips, one is never far from a town of some kind, and any little item that may have been forgotten when selecting the outfit may be purchased later.

Regarding the quality of the goods selected, I advise buying only the best. One does not like the idea of some much needed article giving out when far back in the woods, for such an occurrence may mean considerable annoyance and discomfort. Then, too, there is some satisfaction in the possession of a good outfit, while the cheaper goods always prove unsatisfactory.

Of course, it will be understood that the list of articles mentioned does not cover the field entirely, but the various items which are needed on certain occasions will be mentioned later.

CHAPTER III.

CLOTHING FOR THE WOODS.

HE question of clothing is an important one, for when in the woods the wardrobe cannot be replenished. It is difficult to give advice on this subject, as the field is a large one and climatic and other conditions necessitate a different style of clothing in the various sections where the temperature, etc., are so very unlike. As a general rule I will say adopt the style of clothing which is most generally worn in the particular locality where you intend going. To illustrate my ideas plainly I find that it will be necessary to take up each article separately and tell what I know of its good and bad points.

FOOTWEAR. Everybody who goes into the woods does so with a purpose. It may be for hunting, trapping, fishing, prospecting, canoeing, exploring, or merely for a camping trip, and the various callings, or recreations, sometimes call for different kinds of clothing, especially so with regard to footwear.

For prospecting or exploring in summer or at any time when the ground is bare, also for fishing and bird hunting, I recommend the use of the hunting boot in the lighter grades. There are many of them on the market and they are made with several lengths of tops, to suit the various tastes.

For still hunting, for trapping in spring and fall, and for canoeing, I have never found any-

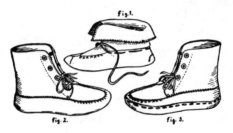

Various Styles of Moccasins.

thing to equal the heavy oil tanned moccasin or pac. (See Fig. 2.) They are waterproof and will remain so if kept well oiled, are light and soft and not likely to slip on rocks and logs, neither are they noisy as are the hunting boots and shoes. They have only a single thickness of leather on the bottoms, but if one desires to get greater wear he may sew on a pair of soles as shown in Fig. 3. They may be sewn on with a strip of rawhide if for use on dry ground, but

if it is desirable to retain the waterproof qualities it is best to use heavy waxed thread. The
leather should be soaked so it will take the proper shape, and the sewing should be done over a
last. These moccasins may be obtained from
almost any sporting goods dealer and in the
North at any shoe or general store.

Those who are not used to wearing soft
shoes or moccasins are likely to be troubled by
sore feet. For such, the soled moccasins are
advised and it will help greatly to fit them with
leather insoles. One will soon get used to the
moccasins and the soreness of the feet will pass
away. Shoe pacs should always be kept oiled
to retain their waterproof qualities.

In some sections of the eastern states, the
rubber shoe is much worn in the spring and fall.
They are indeed a nice article, especially for use
during wet weather. I can recommend the low
ankle shoe with strap and buckle, in "snag
proof" quality. They are not noisy like leather
shoes, and are especially desirable for fall trapping. However, for water trapping the rubber
boot is to be preferred.

In Fig. 1, we have the Chippewa moccasin,
which is by all means the most desirable article
for snowshoeing. They are made of moose, caribou or deer skin, Indian tanned, and can be
obtained only from the Indians. Having cloth

tops, they hold the snowshoe strings securely, and the shape of toe is better than that of the ordinary Sioux pattern moccasin. These moccasins are easily made, and Figs. 4 and 5 show two patterns, the only difference being in the toe. In sewing in the vamp, the sides must be gathered slightly, and if the material is not too heavy it is best to make an inside seam. The heel

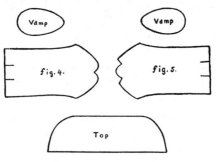

Chippewa Moccasin Pattern.

is made by bringing the edges of the end together, and turning the small flap in the center up over the seam, on the outside. After sewing up, they should be well washed and kept stretched into the proper shape while drying. When dry, the gathering on the sides, will have entirely disappeared.

The oil tanned pac and the factory made moccasins of the same style are what is known

as the Sioux pattern. They are also easily made
if one has the proper material. If you have an
old pair of factory made moccasins, rip them
apart and then you can cut a pattern over them,
making them larger or smaller than the old ones

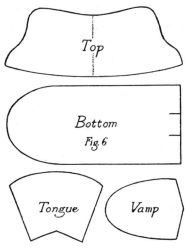

Sioux Moccasin Pattern.

if desired, and remedying all the defects of the
old pair. If you have no old ones, cut the bottom
as shown in Fig. 6, the vamp and tops being
made as shown.

I make a last of the proper size and shape,
of cedar or pine wood, then soak the leather in

warm water and fasten the bottom piece to the
last with small tacks. I first bring up the toe
and tack it to the last, then the sides, then the
slack part between, etc. Don't try to bring the
bottoms too far up, or you will have wrinkles
that you cannot get rid of. It is easier to make
the vamp quite large and thus throw the seam
lower on the toe and sides, then sew the vamp
into place. If the material is very thin, put the
seam on the inside, otherwise have it outside.

Sew on the tops and make a bellows tongue
as shown, sewing it to the tops and vamp the
same as in shoes of this style. You can remove
eyelets fom old shoes and use them for the moc-
asins.

To make a neat moccasin, it should be allowed to dry on the last and when so done it
will take a nicer shape and the gathering in the
sides will disappear.

When dressing the feet, I advise the use of
the ordinary woolen socks, and plenty of them.
Never wear cotton, especially during cold weather. The heavy German socks are very warm but
require too much time in drying. Many people
of the North wear long strips of woolen cloth
wound round the feet. This is all right, but I
prefer an extra pair of socks.

UNDERWEAR AND SHIRTS. Wear only woolen
underclothing. It is warmer than cotton and

absorbs perspiration. I advise the use of the finer grades, the unshrinkable kind being best.

Overshirts should always be of wool. I have always thought that a gray flannel shirt is about the nicest thing that one can find for outdoor wear. It does not show dirt as some colors do, and is not likely to fade as will the blue shirt, which is so much worn.

COATS, TROUSERS, ETC. For bird hunting, fishing, prospecting, and for general outdoor wear, the duck hunting clothing is all right for those who like it, but I do not. It is cold, noisy in the brush, and stiff. I would rather wear corduroy, but Mackinaw cloth is better than either, especially for cold weather. The Mackinaw coat is light, soft and warm, is not noisy, turns a fair amount of water, and is in all ways the most practical article for the big game hunter. In the northern brush it is worn almost exclusively. I like the blue-black color, but in sections where there is much hunting done and hunters (?) shoot at everything they see moving, it is advisable to use something more conspicuous, say red. There is a very nice hooded coat worn by the Hudson Bay trappers, but it can be procured only from the Hudson's Bay Co. It is cut rather long and is kept closed by means of a sash tied about the waist, it has no buttons. The hood is a very nice thing during

extreme cold weather, and it is also good in the
dense evergreen forest, as it prevents the snow
from going down inside the clothing. A hood
made of woolen cloth may be used with an ordinary coat by pinning or tying under the chin,
and will answer the purpose almost as well, and
when not in use may be tucked in an inside
pocket.

But a small number of woodsmen are able
to make their own clothing but I am fortunate
in that respect as I am rather handy with a
needle. I have made my own hunting clothing
on more than one occasion. If one can do such
work he will often be able to make a good coat
from an old woolen blanket, as I have done, and
he can also make shirts and trousers. Very
good and well wearing trousers can be made
from seamless grain bags, the better grade to
be preferred. If you don't like the color, a package of "Diamond Dye" will make them look all
right. It is easily handled. Of course, this is
not for the sportsman but for the real practical
woodsman who has the material and the time
and is not hampered by style and the opinions of
friends. One seldom meets ladies when in the
big woods, anyway.

For those who go out only for a short trip
in summer or fall, any old clothing will do. A

faded or shabby business suit is as good as anything.

HATS, CAPS AND GLOVES. For summer and fall wear an ordinary soft wool hat is the proper thing in my opinion. The lighter grades should be chosen for summer wear, and for the South the stitched white duck hats are excellent.

The corduroy hunting cap is also a fine article for fall and spring wear. I refer to the kind having neck and ear protectors, which tie over the crown. In extremely cold weather I prefer to wear the knitted wool toque. It is light, soft and warm and may be drawn down over the ears as far as desired, moreover, it may be worn at night when camping out, and when on the trail it does not interfere with the use of the pack strap. With one of these toques and a hood such as before mentioned, one can withstand the most severe winter weather.

As for gloves, will say that I have never been able to keep my hands warm in any kind of leather glove or mitten. However, I have worn leather mittens over woolen ones and can recommend such an outfit for cold weather, but for the most part I wear mittens of heavy cloth. They are soft and warm, and if they happen to get wet, may be dried quickly by the side of the fire without danger of burning. They should fit loosely so they can be withdrawn quickly, as, for instance, when one sees game and must make a quick shot. If, however, one wishes to wear leather gloves or mittens, I will say that horsehide is the best wearing leather, with buckskin a close second. The northern Indians wear buckskin mittens with a heavy wool lining, and they either have them fastened by cords to the sleeves of the coat, or they will have them connected with a long knitted cord which is passed over the neck. This prevents the mittens from falling into the snow when removed, for instance, when setting a trap.

It will be understood that the foregoing remarks are based mainly on my own experience, and while I give rules, yet as everybody knows, there are exceptions to all rules, and as regards the matter of clothing, a considerable range of choice is allowed, without departing far from the line that is laid out. On the whole as I stated before it is wise to learn if possible the style of clothing worn in the part where one expects to take his outing, and adopt something of a similar nature.

CHAPTER IV.

pensable
s a rig of
ying or
om place
e various
the most
tisfactory
are the p‌ pack sack
and the pack basket. These devices are in
tended for different kinds of work, and each is
good for the work for which it was designed,
and practically worthless for any other.

The pack strap is used mainly for portaging
on the canoe routes, and is used throughout the
northern forests, almost exclusively for this purpose. The most common type consists of a head
band of rather stiff leather, about two and a half
inches in width by about two feet in length; to
each end of which is attached a strap of the same
kind of leather, from eight to ten feet long. The
straps are attached either by sewing or by means
of rivets, and are cut about one inch wide at the
ends, which are fixed to the head band and taper

35

to about one-half inch at the free ends. The entire length of the strap will be from eighteen to twenty-two feet. The best kind have the

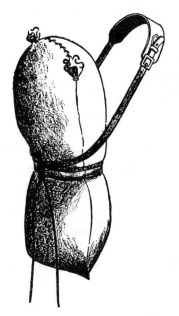

The Pack Strap or Tump Line.

straps buckled to the head band and this kind possess decided advantages over the ordinary kind, for, in case it loosens and stretches out, because of the shifting of the goods in the pack,

it may be quickly adjusted to the proper length
by means of the buckles.

With one of the outfits, all kinds of goods
may be handled readily, whether the pack is a
bag of flour, a barrel, or a box of groceries. It
is used by tying to the pack and not by means of
buckles, and for this reason soft leather, web-
bing, etc., cannot be used. When properly adjusted, the part of the strap which passes over the
head should be of such a length that it will not
have a tendency to draw the head back, and the
pack should rest well up on the back of the carrier. It will be understood that the pack hangs
from the head of the packer and not from the
shoulders. To the uninitiated for the first few
days, this kind of work will be exceedingly tiring, the strain on the head and neck being very
severe, but it is surprising how soon one will become accustomed to it. It is a fact that a heavier
pack can be carried with the head strap than
with shoulder straps; many of the northern Indians being able to handle several hundred
pounds on a short portage, but when the nature
of the goods is such that it may be arranged into
suitable packs, the majority of woodsmen prefer
to make it up into lots of about seventy pounds
and on the short portages will take two packs,
one on the top of the other.

Sometimes the Indians, instead of using the "tump line," adjust a piece of codfish line to each pack, placing a piece of birch bark, or something

Packing with the Tump Line.

on that order, on the head as a protection from the narrow cord. This saves considerable time which would otherwise be consumed in adjusting the strap to the various packs. A barrel of flour will be divided into three equal parts, and placed in square canvas bags, the cord being tied to two of the corners. On a long portage he will take only one pack, but if it is a short distance only, he will throw another one on top, and if the portage is very short he will take three such packs. The average white man, however, will have plenty of trouble with one. The 'tump line" is a very useful article, for it may be put to many uses, other than portaging goods; for instance, it is better than a rope for drawing a toboggan and may also be used for leading the canoe through the rapids, as well as many other purposes which will suggest themselves when one makes camp for the night. It is not good for packing on the trap line or where there is no trail, as one cannot look about to see where he is going, but they are useful just the same and it is well to have one along, always, when traveling in the bush. For instance, one may kill some kind of big game and wish to take the head or a quarter of meat along to camp, or if a trapper, he may have some large animal in a trap and will not have time to skin it on the trail and in all such cases the pack strap will be very useful indeed.

For the trapper who is tending a long line of traps, and always has something to carry with him, also for any person who is going into the woods for a camping trip, making long trips and carrying a light outfit, I recommend the use of the pack sack. As its name implies it is a sack or bag, made of duck, and fitted with both shoul-

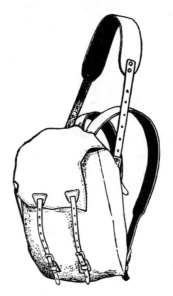

The Pack Sack.

der and head straps, all adjustable. They are much used along the border and in such places may be purchased from any hardware or sporting goods store, but if they are not to be procured, may be made by almost any person who

cares to go to a little trouble. The sack is made
square, about twenty-six or twenty-eight inches

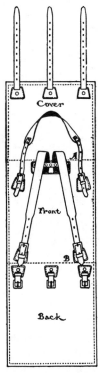

Construction of Pack Sack. To be Folded on Dotted Lines
A and B, and sewn up on edges.

in size and has a flap covering the top
and fastening with three straps and buckles.

The head and shoulder straps are fastened securely to the opposite side and should be made of heavy leather, the shoulder straps being placed very close together at the top, so that there will be no trouble in keeping them in place. Of course, there are good and bad pack sacks, some carrying very nicely and others are continually slipping down on the back and causing trouble, but they are certainly a fine article if rightly made.

When choosing a pack sack, beware of the kind having gussets in the sides and bottom. This kind is sure to carry badly as one cannot make a flat pack of such an arrangement and if the pack projects too far from the back of the carrier, it has a tendency to pull back hard on the head and shoulders.

There are some who do not like the pack sacks, but when you ask them why, and what they use, the answer is never satisfactory, to me at least.

When carrying my camp outfit I always arrange it to bring the blanket next to my back and if I have anything that is likely to be damaged by crushing I place it in the top of the pack. Of course, they are not intended for carrying eggs or glassware but sensible men, as a rule, leave such goods behind them when going into the wilds.

In the eastern states and the eastern provinces of canada, and especially in the Adirondack mountains of New York the pack basket, made

Packing with the Pack Sack.

to fit the back, fitted with shoulder straps and in some cases, with head strap also, is much used.

They are made in various sizes and grades,

the better quality being covered with cotton duck. About all that can be said in favor of the basket is that it offers a greater protection to the goods than does the sack, but as an offset to this good quality it is heavy and cumbersome and because of its shape, brings the weight of the goods too far from the back of the packer.

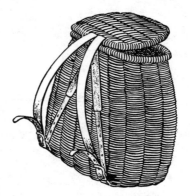

The Pack Basket.

It can only be used for small articles, the size of which will admit of being dropped through the circular top of the basket, but it is nice for carrying frail articles when going on a short trip.

There is also what is known as a pack harness, but I have never given this article a trial. It is made with shoulder straps and is intended to buckle on to any kind of a pack. While I cannot say much either for or against it, having never used it, I believe it would be nice for carrying the camp outfit, etc., providing one does not have occasion to open the pack on the trail, for all such arrangements require too much time for opening and doing up again.

CHAPTER V.

F you desire comfort in camp, and there are few who don't, then I say, give considerable thought to the selection of a camping outfit. There are many very complete camping outfits sold by the sporting goods houses but they are not practical for the woodsmen, in fact, are not made for him, for the camp outfitters cater mostly to the city sportsman. The trouble with these outfits is that they are too complete for every-day use and there are many articles which may be omitted, must be when going far back from civilization. For my part I prefer to go into a hardware store and select a few articles, a few more somewhere else, and so on until my outfit is complete. When finished, no article has been overlooked or forgotten and there is nothing that will not be needed.

COOKING OUTFITS. Of cooking utensils, those most in evidence in the woods, consist mainly of frying pans, camp kettles and tin pails. In choosing these goods, weight is one of the points to be considered, for one does not care to carry heavy stove furniture, and for my use, I select mostly stamped steel and heavy retinned goods. Aluminum is much used for camp kits, but is not generally liked by practical woodsmen. Of course, in selecting a cooking outfit, the size of the camping party must be borne in mind, for when the party is a large one, the largest size utensils must be used, and in order to reduce the bulk as much as possible, the sizes

The Camper's Frying Pan.

should be such that they will "nest" one in the other.

Frying pans should have the handles cut off and a square socket riveted on, as the long handle is always in the way when making up a pack. When in use a wood handle is inserted in the socket and one can use as long a handle as desired. Writers on woodcraft advise always fixing the pan on supports, over a bed of coals, and this is really the proper way, but there are times when for various reasons one prefers to

hold the pan, and it is on such occasions that
the long handle is preferred. For instance, it
may rain, as it often does when one is camping
out, and in cooking over the open fire by the side
of a lean-to camp, the long handle is very nice,
indeed, as it will not be necessary to stand in the
rain in order to reach the fire. On long, hard
trips one naturally wishes to travel as light as
possible, and on such occasions, as I usually
travel alone, I have a very small pan, a No. 0

The Two Man Outfit.

size, fitted with a square socket. I say square,
for a round socket will allow the pan to turn on
the handle unless driven very tightly.

For kettles, I would also advise selecting
something light. The tinned camp kettles are
all right, and as before mentioned, these should
nest, one in the other. Drinking cups should be
of tin, tapering so that they will nest, and the
handles must be open at the bottom. Tin plates
are advised, but if one is fitting up a permanent
camp, the white enameled plates will be found

to be excellent, also enameled cooking ware. A knife, fork and spoon should be taken for each member of the party, also a couple of large spoons. When traveling light, however, I carry no table ware whatever, my hunting knife and a pointed or flattened stick answering for all purposes.

A very nice thing to have when one must cook over an open fire is the tin baker. With one of these, bread or biscuits may be baked by the side of an open fire as well as in an oven. They are made tapering on the top and bottom, thus reflecting the heat towards the center and baking the bread evenly from all sides.

Very good folding bakers may be procured from any camp outfitting firm and in case one does not have ready access to such an establishment, any tinsmith can make one. It will be understood that this is mainly for use in the permanent camp, and if the tinner finds it difficult to make a folding one, a solid one will answer. It should be made of bright, heavy tin plate and the brighter it is kept, the better work it will do.

This baker, however, is not a necessity, as one can do all kinds of baking with a frying pan alone. There are a number of elaborate cooking outfits on the market, but they are expensive and contain many articles which are not needed,

and I would advise going to a hardware store
and selecting goods of the kind mentioned above.
The elaborate outfits carried by some camping
parties have a tendency to lead the guide to use
bad language, but for a large party who employ
a cook and packers, they are all right. The
practical woodsmen, however, are always in
favor of a light and simple outfit. A light cotton bag should be provided, in which to carry
the cooking utensils, and they should always be

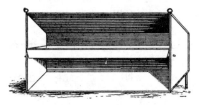

The Folding Baker.

made as clean as possible before placing in the
pack. To clean a greasy frying pan, heat it over
the fire and plunge into cold water, finishing
with moss or grass. Use the largest vessel for
dish washing.

BEDS AND BEDDING. To the one who has
never done any camping, the question of bed
and blankets is one that will set him to wonder-
ing and he will have doubts as to whether he
will be comfortable with the outfits recommended

by those who have been there, but I will say that when camping out, a fire is kept up all night, and in a tent or log camp also, if the weather is cold, then, too, if the party consists of several members they can double up, placing two outfits together. There is considerable difference of opinion among woodsmen, regarding the blanket question, many preferring some one of the various sleeping bags which are advertised by sporting goods dealers, and others preferring woolen blankets or combinations of one kind or other.

For my part, I do not like the sleeping bag. The ordinary sheep-lined bag is heavy and bulky and not as warm as it is supposed to be. If the weather is cold, it will be absolutely necessary to keep a fire at night, and as one must replenish the fire from time to time, the bag will be no end of trouble, for it requires considerable time to fix one's self comfortably in the bag.

For ordinary fall weather, woolen blankets are the proper thing. With a few large safety pins they may be pinned shut on the end so that one will not kick them off his feet and are easy to get into, making no trouble when he gets up to fix the fire. On the trail they are much lighter than the sleeping bag and may be rolled up into a smaller space. A cotton or part cotton blanket should never be used for camping out, as they

are likely to catch fire from sparks from the
camp fire.

On one occasion when camping with cotton
blankets, I was awakened by a feeling of warmth,
and a very rapid investigation revealed an eighteen inch hole burned in my blanket, also one
leg of my trousers badly burned. It is needless
to say that I discarded the cotton blankets after
that experience.

The Hudson's Bay, the Mackinaw and the
U. S. Army blankets are among the best. A
wide single blanket is best, as one can lay on one-
half and use the other half as a cover. Double
bed blankets are not good. I have used a square
horse blanket and found it very nice for camping.

For extremely cold weather, the woven rabbit skin blankets made by the northern Indians
are far ahead of any other thing which I have
ever used. A full sized blanket will weigh, perhaps ten pounds, but is warmer than all the
woolen blankets that one can carry. There is
only one objection to this rig, namely, the hair is
coming out continually, but of course, in the
woods one does not care if he has some rabbit
hair on his clothing. This may be remedied by
covering the blanket with light woolen material,
but the covering adds to the weight without increasing the warmth, in fact, it is my opinion
that the blanket is warmer without it. These

blankets or robes are made only by the northern Indians and have never been placed on the market, but may be procured sometimes, through the Hudson's Bay Company and other northern traders.

Regarding beds, the only one that is much used in the woods is made of balsam or other evergreen boughs. Properly made, they are comfortable, but must be replenished as the boughs become pressed down and the bed becomes hard. Only the lighter tips should be used, and they should be placed with the stems down, commencing at the head of the bed. For a pillow, the extra clothing may be placed in a bag, or a bag may be filled with boughs or dead grass. A bag filled with deer hair makes an excellent pillow, and dry moss is not bad.

A very comfortable bed may be made from the skins of moose, caribou or deer, if one is fortunate enough to have the material on hand. A frame should be made of poles and the hide cut in strips an inch wide, thoroughly soaked and stretched and strung in the frame some three or four inches apart, the strands crossing two ways. After it is dry it will make a very springy bed, and may be covered with deer or other skins, with the hair left on. There are many campers who will not agree with me regarding camp outfits, but I believe that the majority of the "old timers" have views similar to mine, and that any person who has had considerable experience will speak well of a simple outfit.

CHAPTER VI.

FIREARMS.

HE gun question is indeed a perplexing one, for while there are many who will cheerfully give advice on the subject, there are so many brands of firearms, so many different bores and calibers, weights and lengths, and systems of operating, that the novice, after hearing all of the advice, is perhaps as much at a loss as before, and the confusion is not in the least diminished when he considers the many different conditions under which the arm is to be used. While there is all kinds of game to be hunted, there are all kinds of guns to choose from, and there are a number of good guns for each and every kind of hunting, too many, in fact.

There are many who cannot afford to own a number of sizes adapted to hunting both large and small game, therefore they desire an arm for general use, one that may be used for all kinds of shooting and under all conditions. While one hunter will recommend one brand and caliber another will advise the use of something different, therefore the buyer, unless an experienced hunter, will not know whether he has bought the proper arm or not, until he has given it a practical trial and found it satisfactory or the reverse, as the case may be. It is mostly in regard to rifles that there is so much confusion for there are not so many different types and bores of shotguns.

SHOTGUNS. Modern shotguns may be divided into four distinct types, namely: the single barrel breech loader, the double barrel, the hand manipulated repeaters and the automatics. The single barrel gun is not much used by sportsmen, except in the heavy, big bore style for ducks and geese, but it is much used by beginners, young hunters and trappers. Because of its lighter weight it is often the best gun for the trapper especially when the small bores are selected.

There is a single barrel, muzzle loading gun used by the Hudson Bay trappers which deserves mention. It is twenty-four or twenty-eight gauge, has a thirty-inch barrel and weighs four pounds. For the hunter and trapper of that distant region this simple gun answers the purpose admirably. With it he can kill all kinds of small game and by using round balls can kill such large game as moose and caribou at short range. The ammunition is also light and inexpensive.

While I do not recommend a muzzle loading gun, for use in that country there is nothing on the market that can fill the bill just as well. It is true that there are single barrel breech loading guns of the same gauge and weight but they are all choke bored and will not shoot a round ball accurately.

Of the double barrel guns there are many, both of American and foreign make, and as they are all made in the same gauges all of the higher grades give general satisfaction, the choice usually being a matter of preference. Of course, the various gauges and lengths of barrel are designed for different kinds of work. For instance, the duck hunter is inclined to use a rather large gauge, long barrel, choke bored gun, designed for close shooting at long range, while the hunter who makes a specialty of partridge and woodcock, selects a gun of light weight having short cylinder bored barrels, as his hunting is usually in thick brush and game is shot on the wing at short range.

For all around use I would recommend a double barrel, hammerless gun of twelve gauge, twenty-eight inch barrels, right barrel modified choke and left barrel full choke bored, weight seven and a fourth pounds and I believe that any

of the standard American makes will give satisfaction.

The trap shooter is very particular in his
selection of a gun and it is a common practice
to have guns made to order, especially the stock,
which should be of just the proper length and
drop, for in order to do really good shooting the
gun must "fit" the one who is to use it. Such
matters are seldom considered by the average
hunter, and if his gun is of the right gauge,
length and weight, works perfectly and does

The Drop of a Gunstock.

good shooting, he is well satisfied and declares
he has the best gun in the world.

Some hunters do not understand what is
meant by the expression "drop of stock." The
cut will explain this point. To determine the
drop of any gun, lay a straight-edge on the rib,
or barrel, if a single gun, and the measurements between the straight-edge and the stock
at comb and butt gives the amount of drop.
For my use I prefer a gun with a long stock
and not more than 1¾ inch drop at comb and 2½

inches at heel, or butt. Many others prefer more drop than this.

There are some who can do better shooting with the single barrel gun, and they are the ones who use the repeaters. As before said, repeaters are divided into two types, the automatic and the hand manipulated kinds. While one hunter recommends one kind, another insists that the other is the best, but for the prospective purchaser I will say that the automatics are far more rapid than the others, but this is about the only point in which they are superior. The standard guns of this type are choke bored for longest possible range and are much used by duck hunters, but they may also be had in cylinder bore.

The term "bore" or "gauge" is not understood by the average shooter. In times past, all guns were of cylinder bore and were made to shoot round balls. The various sizes were designated by the number of round balls required for a pound, and this is what is meant by the word "gauge." For instance, a sixteen gauge gun, if a true cylinder bore, will use a one ounce ball, sixteen being required for a pound, a twelve gauge takes a twelve to the pound, etc.

The term "choke bore" means that the bore of the gun is constricted, or choked near the muzzle; and this system is used in order to force the shot into a closer bunch, therefore, making a closer pattern and increasing the killing chances at long range.

The choke of a shotgun barrel is all at the muzzle. The term "taper choke" is misleading as the average person thinks that such a gun has a gradual taper from breech to muzzle, but this is a mistake and no guns are bored that way. Such a gun would not throw the shot any closer than a cylinder bored gun would.

The words "cylinder bore" apply to a barrel of uniform gauge, the diameter of the bore being the same in all parts. Such a barrel will give the same penetration as a choked barrel, but will make a larger and more open pattern, and for this reason is preferred for wing shooting in thick undergrowth, where the game must be shot quickly at short range.

RIFLES. Modern sporting rifles may be divided into three distinct types, namely: the single shot, the hand manipulated repeaters and the automatic repeating guns, and these, with the exception of the automatics, may be sub-divided into two styles, differing only in the style of ammunition used, i. e., those using black powder or the equivalent in low pressure smokeless powder and those using high pressure smokeless powder and metal jacketed bullets.

At the present day the single shot rifles are seldom used for big game hunting, but the smaller calibers are much used for shooting small game, also for target use. For this use the .22 caliber is the most popular, both in the single shot and repeating styles, and the .25 caliber is next in order. Both calibers are excellent for hunting such game as squirrels, partridge, woodcock, rabbits and ducks. For those who wish to practice rifle shooting, they are the most desirable sizes, as the ammunition is inexpensive, especially that of the .22 caliber.

All of the American rifle manufacturers make these small bore guns, and all of the higher grades are well made and give satisfaction, thus giving the prospective purchaser a wide range of styles to select from. To parties wishing to buy a rifle of any size, I would advise that they study the catalogues of the various manufacturers, also the "Ideal Hand Book," issued by the Ideal Manufacturing Company.*

Since the small bore craze swept the country, or I might say the world, the large caliber, black powder rifles have become rather obsolete, and the majority of big game hunters use rifles of from .25 to .35 caliber. In some few cases the

---

* This firm has recently passed into the control of the Marlin Firearms Co., New Haven, Conn., to whom all correspondence relating to shooting should be directed.

manufacturers carried the small bore matters to extremes, and of late years, the new styles have been mostly over .30 caliber.

The advantages which the small bore high powdered arms have over the old style are higher velocity, flatter trajectory, lighter weight of both gun and ammunition, almost total absence of smoke and light recoil. These advantages are so apparent that the hunters as a rule discarded their old arms and adopted the new style as soon as they were put out on the market. There are a few, however, who still cling to the black powder gun, claiming that they have greater killing power than the small caliber. While there is no doubt some grounds for the belief, the various advantages of the high powdered gun more than offset this one fault.

The advantages of high velocity and flat trajectory are apparent to all who have given the question consideration, but there are others who say that such extreme powers are not necessary. These parties argue that the game is, for the most part, killed at ranges of less than 200 yards, and that the .44 calibre and even less powerful arms will kill game at such distances. This is true, but high velocity and flat trajectory cannot be developed without the addition of high power. With the high velocity arm, one need make little or no allowance for the distance the game will move during the flight of the bullet, and the comparatively flat trajectory reduces the danger of over or undershooting to a minimum.

The small bore gun has one fault, namely, the rapid falling off in velocity at the longer ranges. Some hunters claim that because of this, the bullet often fails to expand when shooting big game, but personally, I have never had the least trouble in this respect.

For those who have any apprehension with respect to the killing qualities of the small bores, I would advise that they select an arm, using a flat point bullet such as the .30-30 Marlin, the .32-40 and .38-55 high velocity and the .32 Special, as the flat point is more destructive in case the bullet fails to mushroom.

For hunting deer and black bears I can recommend either of the calibres mentioned above, and for larger game such as moose, elk and the large bears of the West and Northwest, I would advise using a more powerful arm, such as the .33, the .30 U. S., the .35 Winchester, etc. For hunting large game in heavy wooded sections, the extra light weight .45-70 Winchester is well liked.

Regarding the various mechanisms, I will say that while I have used the lever action mostly, I can find no fault with the auto-loading guns, and with regard to the different makes will advise that none of the reliable makers will put a gun on the market which is imperfect in action, yet there are many hunters who can find fault with and will condemn every style or brand of arm except the one they are using at the time.

No matter what kind of a rifle is selected it should be equipped with the proper set of sights. Until recent years I used the open rear sight and always thought it was good enough for anybody, but since using the folding peep sight I have found no use for the open barrel sight, and for those who have never used the open peep sight I would advise that they give it a trial. For a front sight to use in connection with the peep, either an ivory or gold bead is good, and I prefer a small bead. As the rifles come from the factory they are all supposed to be accurately sighted, but many hunters will find that a readjustment of the sight will be necessary. The Winchester catalogue gives very plain and complete instructions for sighting firearms.

PISTOLS. Under this heading I include the single shot target pistols, the revolvers and the automatics, as all of these guns are used by woodsmen, to a certain extent.

Throughout the Rocky Mountain region, the revolver is carried as a side arm by many hunters, and even more so by trappers and prospectors. There are times when one cannot be burdened with a rifle, and does not care to go far entirely unarmed. This is often the case with the trapper, as he must sometimes make long journeys, carrying a heavy pack, and quite often he must use an axe and cannot carry the gun. This is where the belt gun comes handy.

A revolver cannot be depended on as much as a rifle, and it is carried mainly as a weapon of defense and for shooting at short range. In choosing such an arm I would advise selecting a large caliber and I prefer a single action gun. The Colt's .45 caliber "Frontier" and "Bisley" models are great favorites. There are also some fine double action guns of .38 caliber, but these are not so much used by hunters, as few like the double action, and the small calibers are not desirable.

It is true that the novice has difficulty in handling the .45 caliber, but when it comes to practical use, extreme accuracy is not sought, but rather a quick shot and good stopping power.

Of late years the automatic pistol has become quite popular with many of the mountain men, and in some ways it is better as a side arm than a revolver. The power and range of some of these arms, such as the Mauser and the Luger is surprising, to say the least, but this good quality is counterbalanced by the awkward "feel" in handling.

There is another style of small arm which is deservedly popular among trappers. I refer to the .22 caliber target pistol. Personally, I have used only the Stevens, Diamond Model, and will say that for the trapper, a better weapon cannot be obtained. Carried in connection with the big game rifle, it is an ideal gun for rabbits, grouse, squirrels, etc., and where such game is plentiful will keep the trap line baited and will also supply considerable food for the trapper. I use the ten inch barrel, equipped with a peep sight and shoot by resting the barrel on my arm, which practically speaking, gives one a rifle in a twelve ounce gun.

Quite recently there has been a small arm put on the market which is almost certain to become popular among the trappers and others. I refer to the Marble's "Game Getter." It is a small combination gun, and is carried in a shoulder holster.

AMMUNITION. The ease with which the modern shotgun ammunition may be reloaded, and the fact that there is such a great difference in results obtained when using the various combinations of powder, shot, wadding, etc., leads the shotgun user to experimenting, and quite often he finds a load that will do better work than the factory loaded ammunition. The careful workmanship of the manufacturers of reloading tools has done much towards perfecting hand loaded ammunition, and the ease and safety with which the bulk smokeless powders may be handled has also helped much to make good results possible. I recommend experimenting in this line, but also advise caution in the use of smokeless powders, especially the dense varieties. Always adhere to the instructions of the powder manufacturers.

I cannot recommend the use of buckshot for any kind of game. Such shot are not deadly enough for any big game, and are entirely too coarse and heavy for any kind of small game. For those who will use them, I will say select a size that will chamber loosely in the muzzle of the gun, and load them in the shell in layers, filling between with very fine soft shot. I have experimented with all styles of loading and find this method the most satisfactory.

To those who use high power rifles, I will say, use factory ammunition for hunting, and it will give good results. If, however, you wish to do your own loading, go carefully, also study the Ideal Hand Book.

For users of the .22 caliber, I advise shooting only the smokeless ammunition with greaseless bullets, especially for hunting, for the lubricated bullet collects dirt and sometimes will not enter the chamber of the gun. The smoke-

less powder does not foul the barrel as black
powder does, and this matter is of some im-
portance to the hunter. The barrel should be
kept well cleaned.

CARE OF FIREARMS. The sportsman, as a
rule, takes good care of his firearms, but there
are others who sadly neglect this important
duty. No matter what kind of a gun you are
using, it should be kept perfectly clean, and
should never be allowed to remain dirty over
night. Even when one is doing considerable
shooting, the residue which accumulates and
remains in the barrels during the day will have a
bad effect in time. This is especially true of
smokeless powders and it is advisable to clean
the barrels on every opportunity, or the burnt
powder will eat into the barrels, forever spoiling
the finish of the barrels, and in case of rifled
arms, sometimes affecting their accuracy.

It is necessary to keep the rifle clean to ob-
tain good results while shooting and this is especially true of the small calibers. The shooting
of the .22 caliber is very much affected by dirt
in the barrel.

The proper way to clean a barrel is from
the breech, but the mechanism of many of the
repeating guns will not allow of this. If it is
necessary to clean a rifle from the muzzle, great
care is advised to prevent injuring the barrel,

as the slightest defect in the muzzle of the gun will seriously affect the shooting qualities.

If dirt has become dry, it will be necessary to use oil to remove it. "Three-in-One" and Marble's "Nitro Solvent Oil" are both very fine, but if the gun is to be set away for some time, it is better to use some heavy gun grease, such as is made by the Winchester, Savage, Stevens and Marlin Companies.

The manufacturers advise keeping the mechanism free of oil during cold weather, but I am not certain whether this is a good idea. I prefer to wipe each part of the action with a slightly oiled rag, for if no oil is used, the gun will draw damp and rust after it is brought into a warm room. If no oil is used it is best to keep the gun out of doors whenever possible.

For all persons taking firearms into the woods, I advise also taking a jointed cleaning rod, some white cotton cloth for cleaning and a bottle of some good gun oil.

CHAPTER VII.

HUNTING KNIVES AND AXES

NE of the most useful articles in the hunter's, trapper's, camper's or prospector's outfit is the sheath knife, and I am sorry to say there are some who condemn this very useful tool. I am inclined to think those who have no use for a sheath knife have never been fortunate enough to own a really good one, and a poor knife is an abomination, far worse than none at all.

The ordinary so-called "hunting knife," such as many sportsmen carry, is of no use whatever in the work for which the hunting knife is intended. The knife which I have shown in the illustration is used everywhere and displayed so universally in hardware and sporting goods stores, and illustrated so much in sporting goods catalogues, that we see it in our mind's eye whenever we hear the words "hunting knife." This knife, if it may be called such, is always a cheap affair and poorly made. It is mostly blade, about one-third of which is point, is thick and

70

heavy with a slender, poorly shaped handle and that very ornamental but useless and bothersome appendage—a guard.

Such a knife is of no account for dressing game, and certainly is worthless as a skinning knife. It will not even slice bread or bacon, the guard is always in the way and prevents the use of a deep sheath, the handle is too small and badly shaped to be held firmly, and as a rule, the temper is such that one must be continually

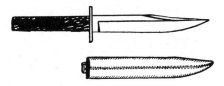

The Common Style of Knife.

using the sharpening stone. Anyway, because of the short sheath with its narrow belt loop, the knife is swinging around continually so that one is almost certain to lose it on the first trip and should consider himself fortunate if he does so.

I prefer a rather small knife, having no guard, and a deep sheath from which only the end of the handle projects. The accompanying illustration shows the knife and sheath which I own at present, and which is my favorite style. This

knife was made by Joseph Rogers & Son, Shef-
field, Eng., and while they are seldom carried in
stock by American dealers, very similar knives
are sold by the sporting goods dealers. The
length of the knife over all is 9 inches, blade
4½ inches, cutting edge 4 inches, thickness on
back about 5-32 inch, with a straight bevel from
near the back to the edge. The point is the
best shape for general use and is excellent for
skinning. It has a nicely shaped, hand-fitting,

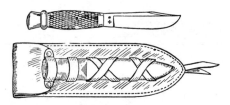

My Favorite Hunting Knife and Sheath.

ebony handle, deeply checked, with a knob on
the end for drawing the knife from the sheath.

The sheath which accompanied the knife
was of the ordinary kind, with a narrow belt
loop on the back. Not liking this arrangement I
fitted the sheath to a leather back, as shown in
the cut, making it somewhat on the order of a
Mexican sheath, and I find this style about perfect. The knife fits snugly in the sheath and
only the end of the handle projects, so that there

is no danger whatever of losing it, and the sheath always stays at the proper place on the belt, never swinging around and turning upside down, as the ordinary kind are likely to do.

For such a knife one will find many uses other than dressing game and skinning furbearing animals. To the camper it is an exceedingly handy article, and may be used for slicing bacon and bread, whittling shavings for starting the fire, and many other uses, in fact, when one becomes accustomed to the use of it he will miss it very much if he does not have it with him. On the trap line especially the convenience of the sheath knife is apparent. When setting traps in cold weather one frequently finds use for a knife, and to pull off a glove and search in a pocket for the jackknife, and then open and use it with rapidly stiffening fingers is far from pleasant. With a knife such as I have described, it is not necessary at all to remove the gloves, and the deeply checked handle offers a firm grip even when the hands are cold and the fingers powerless.

Another very good knife is the "Expert" made by the Marble Safety Axe Co. This knife is lighter than the ordinary hunting knife and therefore, in my opinion, is to be preferred. It also has a very nice shape to both blade and handle.

Even more useful and more necessary than the knife is the hunting axe, in fact, an axe of some sort is indispensable to the trapper and camper, and it should be selected with care, especially when one is going into the wilderness on a camping trip, and must depend on a fire for comfort at night. For the trapper of the bush, the axe is a necessary article; the most useful and necessary item of the outfit. While trapping in the northern bush I have gone for weeks without a gun, but my axe was with me always,

Marble's "Expert" Hunting Knife.

and it was in use almost continuously, for blazing trails, setting traps and cutting the night supply of firewood.

Axes for the outer may be divided into two classes—the light belt axe or hatchet and the heavier camp axe. For those who hunt, trap or fish from home and never camp out at night, the light belt axe is all that is required. There are a number of these hatchets on the market, such as the "Damascus Hunting Hatchet," the "Marble Safety Pocket Axe," and others of less note, and one should have no difficulty in selecting the proper tool. A hatchet of 1¼ pounds is about the right size for general use. I purchased a No. 4 Marble axe, the wood handle style, but not liking the handle and the folding guard, I inserted a 15-inch handle, somewhat heavier than the original, and having very little curve. I wound the handle for six inches of its length, with heavy waxed twine, to give it a better grip, and discarded the folding guard, as I prefer to carry the axe in a leather sheath attached to my belt. This certainly makes an ideal axe for setting traps, dressing game, etc., and I could wish for nothing better for such use.

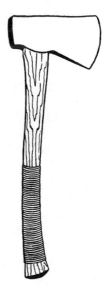

A Remodeled Pocket Axe.

A small belt axe is very useful when on fishing or outing trips in the summer. Did you ever, when fishing, try to reach some very likely looking spot on the pool and find that there was a very obnoxious limb in the way which prevented you from landing the fly in the proper place? If so, you will realize how useful a belt axe would be on such an occasion, for a single stroke of the axe would clear the way. And it is useful on other occasions, for instance, when eating your lunch on a chilly day you will want a fire and the little axe would soon provide fine dry wood.

But such an axe is of no account when making long journeys and camping out at night, especially in the North where the nights, during the hunting and trapping season, are extremely cold and one must keep a roaring fire all night. To camp under a leanto with comfort on a cold night, nearly a half cord of good, dry wood will be needed. When the days are short it frequently happens that after a suitable camping place is found but an hour of daylight remains in which to pitch the camp, prepare a bed, and gather a supply of wood for the night. This means that one must have a good chopping axe and the ability to use it, otherwise it will mean a night of discomfort to say the least.

For such use I select an axe of about two or two and a half pounds weight and fit it with a handle of about thirty inches. This may seem like a long handle for such a light axe, but I have used heavier axes and shorter handles, also short handles in light axes, but find the style described to be most satisfactory.

In selecting an axe one can readily discern all of the good and bad qualities with the exception of that most important one — the temper. There is no way to determine whether an axe is tempered too hard or not hard enough, until one gives it a trial, or at least grinds it, and quite often one finds that the one he has

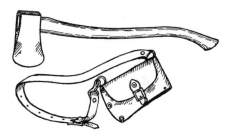

The Camp Axe and Sheath.

selected will not answer his requirements. The only thing to do is to procure another, for one should never take a poor axe into the wilderness, where his comfort and sometimes his life will depend on his axe. An axe that is too hard will break in hard or frozen wood or knots, and a soft axe will bend at the edge. Both extremes are to be avoided, but it is better to have one that is a little softer than the ordinary than the reverse, for one cannot take a grindstone along and will have to depend on the file and small whetstone for sharpening.

The limbs and knots of certain kinds of trees are very hard and they are likely to cause an axe to break or bend and of these the hemlock and the balsam are perhaps at the top of the list and should be given as wide a berth as possible. No matter what the kind of wood may be, if one is far from civilization and has only the one axe to depend on, he should use extreme care in handling it, for to break the axe during cold weather is a serious thing, and one should learn to handle the tool in the proper way. There is also great danger from the axe, in fact, I consider it more dangerous than the gun. Always before striking a blow see that there is no limb or brush in the way which might turn the axe and give you a nasty cut. One must also learn to chop close to the ground without striking into the stones. I have used an axe daily for months without nicking the edge, keeping it in good condition by an occasional use of the whetstone. The secret is in learning to strike the spot aimed at, and in holding the axe rigid; however, this requires practice.

Trappers, as a rule, are good axemen, especially those of the North, but there are many others who know practically nothing of the use of an axe and of falling timber, and for the benefit of such I will give a few instructions.

All trees lean more or less in one direction or other and are inclined to fall that way, but may be thrown to either side where there are no other standing trees in the way, and the first thing noticed by the woodsman is the "hang" of the tree he proposes to cut. If there is nothing to interfere with its falling in the direction in which it leans, he chops a notch on that side, cutting away half the thickness of the tree or until the heart is reached, and then cuts a similar notch on the opposite side, a little higher up, keeping the cut parallel with the first notch so that there will be a uniform thickness of wood to break when the tree commences to fall. If there is no contrary wind the tree is certain to fall in the desired direction.

The wind has great influence over a falling tree and when there is not much lean to the tree and the wind is blowing srtongly one should throw the tree to leeward, as it is almost certain to fall that way. The weight of the limbs also has considerable influence and if the tree appears to stand perfectly perpendicular and the bulk of the limbs are on one side it is safe to say the tree will fall to that side providing there is no contrary wind blowing.

When conditions are favorable and it is desired to do so, one may fell a tree to either side of its incline by notching first on the side towards which it is desired to have the tree fall and cutting the notch on the opposite side several inches higher, bringing the notches close together on the side towards which the tree leans and leaving considerable wood to break on the opposite side.

As before mentioned, all this is well known to the woodsman, but to those who live in sections where there is little or no timber these few instructions may start one on the right track if he should happen to some time locate in the great bush.

Axes, as they come from the factories, have a decided bevel near the edge and a new axe is of no account until it has been well ground. The proper way to grind an axe is to start well back on the blade and grind it out to the edge, or until all of the bevel has disappeared then it should be well whetted with a small, smooth stone. The thickest part of the blade should be not exactly in the center, but somewhat towards the outside corner, that is, the corner that is farthest from the axeman when the tool is in use. An axe so shaped will spring the chip nicely and will not bind in the wood.

For keeping the axe sharp when in the woods, I carry a small, flat, mill file of six or eight inches in length and a small axe stone. A carborundum stone with coarse and fine sides is best for the purpose.

CHAPTER VIII.

UTDOOR life calls for a shelter of some kind and the canvas tent is the thing to use for all ordinary hunting, prospecting, fishing and trapping trips, lasting for a few days to a month; for a greater length of time I advise the use of a log cabin. This for the North, but for the trapper and outer of the central, western and southern states, a good tent with a sheet iron camp stove will make a good home for the entire season. Especially for the trapper, who is likely to desire to move camp occasionally, the tent will be found to be an excellent camp. When trapping on the rivers with a boat, one can set a tent up almost anywhere along the shore in a few minutes and if the trapping is found to be less profitable than expected it is an easy matter to move on a few miles for it only requires a short time to break camp. Anyway the trapper who follows this tyle of trapping moves camp frequently as he

82

makes it a rule to only trap a few nights in any one place.

For prospecting, fishing, pearling or hunting and all other outdoor pursuits where it is desired to have a portable camp, a good tent is all that is required in fact, is all that one could desire.

By the above, I do not mean to say that the tent is not good for the North and for the cold winter weather, far from it. I have known of people spending the entire winter in tents when the temperature remained below the zero point for weeks at a time. With a good tent pitched in a sheltered spot where it will be protected from the storms, well banked with snow and fitted with a good stove, one may defy the Frost King indefinitely.

It is true that the tent has some disadvantages as compared with more substantial shelters such as log and board cabins. Of their faults, frailty is perhaps the most in evidence. One cannot lean against the walls or drive nails on which to hang clothing, etc., as he would in a cabin. When it is raining one must be careful not to touch the roof or he will start it to leaking, unless it is specially treated to make it perfectly waterproof.

But as an offset to these bad qualities the tent is easily transported from place to place,

The Wall Tent.

may be carried on the back if desired, is quickly set up and may be used where a permanent camp would be entirely out of the question.

There are many styles of tents on the market and the most common types are the wall tent, the miner's tent, the Sibley tent and the various styles of leanto shelter tents. For ordinary use I recommend the wall tent, as it is most convenient in form and gives plenty of room.

A wall tent, size 9½ x 11½ feet with 3½ foot walls will be about the right size for two persons. I prefer one made of 8 oz. duck, for it is lighter and that is something worth considering, especially if one must do much packing. In use the light weight tent will usually be found to be as comfortable as the heavier grades.

The tent should have a "sod cloth" extending all around the bottom of the wall, and for comfort I would also recommend a "floor cloth." Some campers also like to use a "fly", and this will be found to be a very desirable article, but it is not at all necessary. I like a tent with loops on the top so that it may be pitched as shown in the illustration. The ordinary kind has an inside ridge pole and two upright supports, one at each end. This style necessitates the carrying of poles which will not go on the trail.

There must also be a stove pipe hole, protected by a sheet of tin having an oblong opening for the pipe. This piece of tin is sewn to the canvas as shown in the cut.

When selecting a camp site one should choose a slight elevation where the ground is perfectly dry and falls away from the tent on all sides. This will insure perfect drainage during wet weather. It is best to have shelter and if a place can be found where a heavy growth of

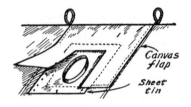

Stovepipe Accommodation.

trees will form a windbreak, so much the better, but one must be certain that there are no big trees which are likely to be blown over and fall on the camp. If there are any such standing near the spot selected they should be felled before pitching the tent. There must also be a bountiful supply of good firewood within easy reach and good, pure water.

The tent should be so pitched that the entrance will be to leeward of the prevailing winds.

It should be well stretched and during damp or wet weather the material as well as the ropes will shrink considerably and should be slacked. In winter it will be necessary for one to select a sheltered spot and also provide in other ways for the cold. Where the snow falls deep one may add much to the comfort of the tent by laying a thick layer of evergreen boughs against the walls and banking well with snow. The filling of boughs will make an air space which is a great frost resister, and will also prevent the melting of the snow from the warmth of the interior.

There are many excellent camp stoves on the market, and if one is using a tent in winter he should have a good stove, as it will be necessary to keep a fire continually. Some of these stoves fold up into a small package and at first thought one would be inclined to select one of that style, but it is well to know that the folding stove has some faults. When new they work perfectly, but after they have been used for some time they become warped by the heat, and if taken apart it will be found to be difficult and sometimes impossible to put them together again. For my own use I prefer an ordinary stove with an oven unless I have a baker, in which case the oven is not needed, and there will be a larger fire box so that one can use longer wood. The stove pipe should be telescopic and of sufficient length to reach three or four feet above the roof of the tent. It will be necessary to have a cone shaped spark catcher made of wire cloth to fit on top of the pipe and prevent sparks from falling on the roof of the tent. Some campers prefer to have the stove pipe hole in the end of the tent instead of the roof, in which case the stove pipe extends diagonally through the end of the tent. This is not only as a safeguard against fire but also precludes all possibility of a leaking place about the stovepipe hole.

There are some good styles of tents other than wall tents, and one of these is the round Sibly tent, which requires only a center pole or may be used with three outside poles. The miner's tent is much used in the west. This tent requires only three poles for pitching. For the trapper who is inclined to travel lightly, there is only one tent to use for the long line, where one seldom spends two nights in succession on the same camp site. That is the shelter tent or leanto.

Various styles of this article have been placed on the market, but I will confess I have never used any of them and therefore do not know their worth. I prefer to make one for my own use, and have made and used several such. The illustration shows the style. A convenient size for one person is 5 x 7 feet; for two it should be somewhat larger. Triangular corners are sewn to each end, and when the shelter is pitched at the proper angle these pieces effectually close the ends. It is best to have a ten inch sod cloth to prevent the wind from entering at the bottom. As it is desired to have this

The Leanto.

shelter very light I made one of drill after having used the heavier duck and found that the lighter material was to be preferred.

In using this tent the open side must always be to leeward of the wind and a fire must be kept burning in front. It is best to find two small trees to which to fasten the ridge pole, but if two cannot be found one will answer, and the other end may be supported by two stakes crossed and lashed to the pole. A good bed of evergreen boughs should be placed inside and a small log may be placed along the open side. The fire should be about six feet distant.

Whenever possible I find it best to build the fire against a large log, and I even fell a green tree sometimes and use it for a fire-back. This log reflects the heat into camp and it also holds fire for a considerable length of time. When a log cannot be used I always, if possible, arrange the camp so as to have a bank of earth or a large rock against which to build the fire.

When the snow comes deep in winter one will have to make a bed of green logs on which to build the fire, for to scrape away three or four feet of snow is out of the question. Small logs of six or eight inches are all right, but they should be of very sappy wood, such as balsam. Placed close together on hard packed snow they will support the fire all night. The snow, where the shelter is pitched, must also be tramped solid with the snowshoes. In such a camp, with a rabbit skin blanket and a good fire, one may sleep comfortably on the coldest night, and even with woolen blankets one can stand considerable frost.

Besides the tents described there are other shelters which may be constructed in case one

is caught out without a place to spend the night.
During the summer months, one can always
make leantos of bark. Cedar bark is excellent
for that purpose. Sometimes one can find a
number of hollow logs which may be split
through the center and will make a perfectly
waterproof roof. The first layer is placed with
the hollow side up and another set of these
scoops are placed hollow side down, over the
cracks. At other times evergreen boughs may
be used and they should be placed thickly,
shingle fashion. These methods of camping are
not for general use, but it is well to know them,
for one never knows when the time will come
when such knowledge will be of value.

CHAPTER IX.

PERMANENT CAMPS.

OR those who desire to move camp frequently, the tent and similar shelters are "the right thing in the right place," but for those who wish to spend an entire season in the same local- ity, a more substantial camp is needed, and the log cabin is recommended. For the wilderness trapper especially such camps are most desirable, and in the more northern dis- tricts where the winters are severe it is almost impossible for the trapper to exist without at least one good, warm, log camp. This camp would be his headquarters, and in it he would store his supplies and his furs, where they would be protected from the elements and the wild creatures of the forest.

In my years of hunting and trapping I have made a number of these camps, and the style which I describe here is my favorite. If well made it is comfortable in all kinds of weather, and it certainly is not a bad place to spend a cold night.

When it is proposed to build such a cabin, the first thing is to select the proper place for the camp site. If it is a trapping camp and the trapper does not intend to have any other sub-

A COMFORTABLE LOG CAMP.

This was a Fishing Camp, 12x12 Feet, but was Used by the Author for a Trapping Cabin.

stantial shelters, it should be located as nearly as possible in the center of the trapping ground, so that one may run out lines in every direction. It is a common practice among the trappers, and especially among those of the western mountain ranges, to build a line of camps, of which one will be the home and base of supplies,

ONE OF THE AUTHOR'S TRAPPING CAMPS.

This Cabin was made in Midwinter. It had a shed roof covered with Tar Paper and the Walls were Chinked with Rags and Pounded Cedar Bark.

and this cabin is, as a rule, the one nearest to civilization. It should be large and roomy and it should be the object of the builder to make it as comfortable as possible.

No matter what the camp may be, it should always be located where there is an abundance of good dry wood. If in the North or West, where the snow falls deep, there should be a good supply of dead standing timber which may be cut after the fallen trees are buried under the snow. Good drinking water is also necessary. The camp should be placed in a sheltered spot and a slight elevation should be selected.

A cabin measuring 10x12 feet inside will be large enough for two persons, and will be more easily kept warm than a larger one. For one of that size the logs should be cut into lengths of 13 and 15 feet, which will allow 18 inches at each end for joining. On the side where the doorway is to be the logs will be shorter, their length depending on just where the door is to be placed. After laying the first round of logs, a place should be cut about 4 inches deep in one of the logs and the door frame should be placed in and nailed securely. This door frame is made of split or hewn wood.

The most simple and satisfactory method of notching the logs at the corners is the one shown in the cut. In order to keep the walls of a uniform height the logs should be of nearly the same thickness. On the side where the door is to be, the logs should be chopped off square on one end, so that they may be butted against

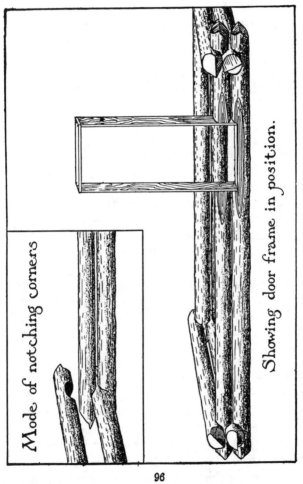

Mode of notching corners

Showing door frame in position.

Method of Building Walls.

the door frame and fastened with large nails. This mode of construction should be followed until the side walls are of the proper height, about 6 or 6½ feet. If possible the log coming directly over the doorway should be so fitted that it will be necessary to cut a section some 3

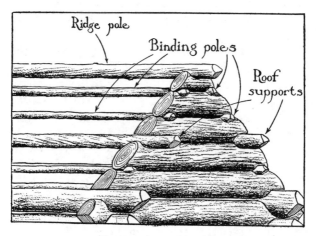

Construction of Gables.

or 4 inches in depth from the log so that it may be fitted over the door frame. This will give greater strength to the walls and prevent the corners from shifting. The logs should all be fitted as closely together as possible, to leave smaller cracks between.

7

The construction of the gables is plainly shown in the cut. The long poles which are used to bind and stiffen the ends should be straight and of an even thickness. The ridge pole should be about 8 or 10 inches in diameter. After the cabin is finished, these poles make excellent supports for shelves on which to store goods, or from which to suspend bags of food, furs, etc.

Material for roofing is what puzzles the amateur woodsman, and I will say that some of the finest roofing material is to be found in the woods, namely, the bark of the trees. Cedar bark is the best, and it should be placed about 3 plys thick, but where it is not to be had, birch, spruce, hemlock, or in fact almost any kind of bark that will peel well may be used. To prevent it from curling it should be well weighted with sods and stones or it may be nailed to the poles.

If the roof supports are some distance apart, it will be necessary to first make a roof of small poles, and if it is desired to make the roof very warm it may be covered with moss before putting the bark on. The only objection to the use of moss is that it makes a delightful home for mice, and they are certain to avail themselves of the opportunity by making nests there.

Although a bark roof is more easily constructed than other kinds, it may be made only during the summer months, anyway the bark must be peeled at that time. Most of the trapping camps are made later in the season when bark is not available, therefore some other material must be used.

A very good, durable roof may be made of troughs or scoops, if one can find some nice splitting wood, and when it is necessary to make

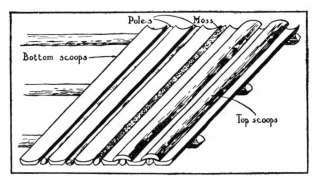

Construction of Scoop Roof.

a roof of this kind the camp should be located only where such wood is to be found. Cedar, balsam, poplar, chestnut and basswood are all free splitting woods. The trees could be cut to the proper length, split through the center and hollowed out, trough shape, on the flat side. This is easily done by cutting notches on the flat side of the stick, leaving the edges stand and splitting out the sections between the notches. A layer of these troughs are placed hollow side up, with a straight pole between each set. This pole is well covered with moss so as to effectually close the crack. Another set of the troughs are then turned hollow side down over the cracks. One large trough is placed over the ridge.

A stovepipe hole must be left at the proper place and half of the hole should be cut from each of one set of scoops. This hole must be several inches larger than the stovepipe it is expected to accommodate so that there will be no danger of fire, and a collar of tin with an upturned edge is placed around the pipe to hold it in place and prevent the ingress of rain.

The door of the cabin may be made of split and hewn boards, and suspended on wooden hinges as shown in the illustration. It is advisable to fasten these hinges together before nailing them to the door. I prefer to have the door swing inward, for sometimes a fresh snowdrift will effectually prevent an outside door from opening.

All cracks between the logs should be tamped full of dry moss. Moss used in this way is far warmer than plaster. I find the moss growing on rocks and logs to be better than that from the marshes, as it is tougher and will stand

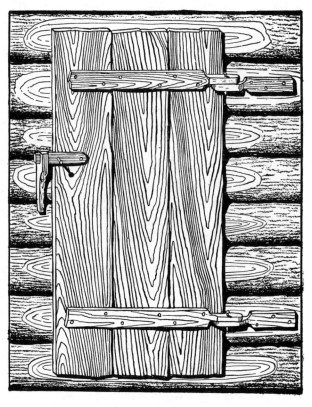

The Door, with Wood Latch and Hinges.

101

handling better. A floor may be made of small, straight poles.

It is almost impossible to take window glass far back into the woods, and for that reason trapping shanties seldom have windows. It is best, however, to have a window whenever pos-

ANOTHER TRAPPING CABIN.
This was a Home Camp and had a Roof of Scoops.

sible, and if glass is not to be had, a piece of parchment (grained deerskin) will make a fair substitute. In a dark camp there is a continued strain on the eyes and one is likely to ruin them in time. Snow blindness is also more likely to occur when this matter is neglected.

For comfort, one should have a table, and a stationary one may be arranged along one side of the cabin. In a previous chapter I gave a description of a good camp bed. In case one cannot procure the materials for a bed of that kind, an ordinary "bunk" of poles may be constructed in one corner of the room. If possible, it should be lined with bark to prevent the balsam needles from falling through, and the space underneath may be used for storing stretching boards and other articles. For heating and cooking purposes I prefer a stove to a fireplace, as it is more comfortable and does not require so much wood.

While the double sided roof is easily made there are some who do not think so or perhaps they would rather have a camp with a shed roof. In building such a camp one should place all of the large logs on one side to make one wall higher than the others. Poles may then be placed on, pointing to the low side and the whole roofed with bark. If one is not too far from town, this, as well as any other kind of log camp may be roofed with tar paper or what is better, tar felt.

There are times when the stove is out of the question, as when one goes a long distance into the woods. In such cases a fireplace must be used. A common way of arranging an open fireplace is by leaving in the center of the roof a large square hole and surmounting it by a split board chimney. The fire is simply placed on the ground floor in the center of the camp and the

The Collier's Shanty — Before and After Roofing.

smoke allowed to escape overhead, if it is so inclined, which by the way is seldom the case unless one has used special care in selecting a camp site. Just what kind of a place should be selected for a comfortable camp of this kind I am unable to say, as I have never had a comfortable camp of that style. One thing is certain —there must be no high hills or mountains near, for in case there are any the wind will persist in tumbling down through the chimney and scattering the smoke all through the camp.

One of the very best fireplace camps that I know of is the style that was formerly used by the cordwood choppers on the Alleghany mountains when charcoal furnaces were in vogue, and which were known as "collier's shanties". They are always very narrow, never more than 7 feet in width, and the fireplace occupies one entire end. The logs are placed exactly as in the cabin above described, until the walls are about 4 feet in height, when a second wall is started across the end where the fire place is to be, and about 2 feet from the end of the camp. This double gable is continued in the form of a chimney and the ridgepole is butted into it. When finished, the end of the camp is lined with large stones for a height of several feet, forming a fireplace directly under the chimney, which is plastered inside with clay. The bed is placed in the opposite end of the camp and the doorway is always at one side and near the fireplace. These camps never have any floors.

I have seen a camp built against a perpendicular rock, which formed a fireback, and no chimney was required. The camp was made with a shed roof and a two foot opening extended across the roof alongside of the rock, allowing the egress of the smoke. Such shelters are all right for use along the trap line and in which to spend a night occasionally, and need not be made very large.

The Indians invariably use the wigwam, or tepee. It was perhaps the most simple style of habitation that the prehistoric man could think of, so it was adopted and has been used ever since. They are made of bark over a framework of poles, are cone shaped, and roof and walls are one. The chimney is simply a hole in the highest part of the roof and the doorway is a hole in the side, closed by a piece of canvas, a gunny-sack or a deer skin. They must be constructed during the summer, as it is only at that time the bark can be peeled from the trees. Birch bark is used mostly, and if it is desired to have it sewn together it must be done at once as the bark will curl awfully when it commences to dry. The bark should be cut an even width and sewn into strips about 10 feet in length, using tmarack or spruce roots for the sewing. Where bark is plentiful and it is never necessary to move camp it is not sewn together, but is

Some Western Hunting Camps.

107

placed shingle style over the poles and held there by placing other poles over it.

Like the open fire camp the wigwam is always smoky, and they are also cold. I have heard of the western Indians arranging a wind shield over the smoke hole, thus causing a draught and removing much of the smoke that would otherwise spread about the interior. It is my opinion, however, that such camps can never be as comfortable as log cabins.

Although most of the wigwams are of a rounded form, I have also seen square ones, and I believe the square one is better as it gives more room. It is also more easily constructed as the bark will fit well on the flat sides of the pyramid shaped structure. For such a camp, a three foot wall of logs should be made and the poles leaned over the wall.

Who of the young trappers has not at one time dreamed of some day going off into the wilds where game is plentiful, and there constructing a fine cabin from which to wage war against the game and furbearing animals. I will confess that I have done so many a time and then I would plan that cabin. How neat and how conveniently arranged every detail of that camp! Every article of the outfit had its place, and of course, was always supposed to be there. Now there is no reason why the camp should not be just like that, if one has the time to fix it up to his liking.

For the sake of cleanliness, there should be a floor (not too near the fireplace) and it should be kept clean by sweeping occasionally with a bunch of evergreen boughs. There should also be a table of fair size, a cupboard or mouse proof grub box and plenty of shelves.

The poles used for binding the eaves make excellent supports for shelves, and if desired, one may make a ceiling over a part of the room, the space above being very convenient for storing the outfit. There should also be plenty of nails or wooden pegs driven into the wall on which to hang clothing, guns, cooking utensils, etc.

Outside one may build a bake oven of stones and clay, and a shed in which to cure furs and store fresh meat. Many other things will suggest themselves after one has commenced operations, and if he so desires he may have an abundance of work to keep him out of mischief until the active season opens.

CHAPTER X.

ANOES and boats of one kind or another are used by all progressive, up-to-date hunters, trappers, fishermen, pearlers and others, who are fortunate enough to reside in a locality where watercraft can be employed. In many parts of the country successful trapping could not be prosecuted without their aid, and for all of those who fish for market, hunt pearls or shoot ducks along the streams and lakes of the South, the boat is indispensable. In the North, the boat is replaced by the lighter, easier running canoe, for there the waters are rough and the craft as well as the outfit must be carried around rapids and falls and from one lake and stream to another.

I have myself done some trapping on one of the southern rivers and found the boat a necessity. The one I used there was only 12 feet in length, and I found it too small. Afterwards I helped to make several other and better ones.

MAKING HUNTING BOATS. For duck hunting and for trapping mink and muskrats on lakes and rivers where the water is not too rapid, I recommend a boat of the following dimensions: Length over all 15 feet, length of bottom 14 feet, width of bottom just forward of center 27 inches (widest part), width across gunwales at stern 25 inches, 5 inch flare at stern (end and sides), 6 inch flare at center, 7 inch at bow; to be made of $\frac{1}{2}$ or $\frac{3}{8}$ inch pine or basswood lumber, over an oak frame. The boat will have some curve to the bottom and will be a light, graceful, easy-running craft; to be used with oars, paddle or pole, as conditions require.

When making such a boat the first step is the selection of the lumber. It should be strictly first class, free from knots and flaws. Boards of a length of 16 feet will be required for the sides, for although the bottom is only 14 feet in length the flare at the ends will require a foot or more, and the curve of the sides will also gain somewhat on the length. Two 14 inch boards will make the bottom, but if they cannot be had in that width, 3 narrow ones will do; 12 inch boards will answer for the sides.

There must also be a 12 inch board of 1 inch thickness, from which to make stern end, seats, etc. The material for the frame must be straight grained and free from flaws or knots; about $1\frac{1}{2}$ or 2 inches is the right size. A few other pieces of 1 inch boards will be needed in making up a

form on which to build the boat, but any old
lumber will answer for that.

The lumber having first been planed the bottom should be cut out carefully and made up
with cross strips as shown in Fig. 1. These
strips, 11 in number, should be placed 14 inches
apart, from center to center. They will stand
up two inches from the bottom, at the edges,

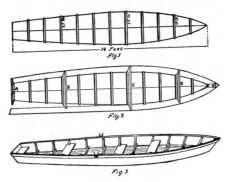

Construction of Boat.

but may be cut down to one inch in the center,
which will leave the bottom smoother.

The stern piece (A. in Fig. 2) is next made
and nailed firmly to the bottom. It is cut from
the one inch board and will measure 12 inches
wide by 15 inches on one edge and 25 inches on
the other, which will give an even bevel or flare
of five inches on each end.

Three similar pieces should be cut (B.B.B. Fig. 2) and fastened to the cross strips as shown. The first one, counting from the stern, should measure 21 inches on one edge by 32 inches on the other. This will make the flare 5½ inches at each end, and it should be fastened in place on the third cross strip from the stern.

The next board should be placed on the fourth cross piece, forward of the first board, which is the widest part of the boat and should measure on one edge the same as the width of the bottom at that point, the top being 12 inches longer, which gives a 6 inch flare at each end.

The third cross board should be attached to the second strip from the bow and should have a flare of 5 inches at each end. The old lumber is used for these forms, for they will be removed when the boat is finished.

A triangular shaped strip of hardwood (C, Fig. 2) should be nailed carefully in the bow, giving it a 7 inch slant forward, and the ends of the side boards should be securely fastened to it, either by nails or what is better, wood screws. The boards are then drawn in and fastened to the flaring cross boards, and lastly should be nailed securely to the stern piece. It will be found that in order to bring the edges of the sides down firmly against the bottom of the boat — and this is necessary — the bottom will have to be curved upward at the ends, or in other words, it must be given a rocker shape.

This may be easily accomplished by allowing the ends only, of the boat, to rest on some solid objects, and by putting some weight in the center the bottom will take the proper shape and the sides will fit up nicely. Nail the boards to the bottom as you go along, using ¾ or 1 inch wire nails. Fig. 2 illustrates this stage of the construction.

The next step is to nail 12 inch strips upright on the inside of the boat, one to each cross-strip of the bottom. They should be nailed firmly to the cross strips and then to the sides. These braces must be 2 inches wide at the bottom but may taper to 1 inch at the top. The board forms (B.B.B.) may then be removed, and a strip of wood ½ by 2 inches should be nailed along the edges of the boat on the outside. Some use a square strip about one inch in diameter.

Seats and oar locks may then be made and put in place and all cracks filled with white lead, the whole given a good application of raw linseed oil, and after it has dried, several coats of paint. When the paint has dried the boat is ready for use. Figure 3 shows the finished craft.

For the trapper's boat I recommend bow-facing oar locks. By their use he will sit facing the bow and can see and avoid the projecting willows, snags, etc., when running close along shore, looking at traps. It is inconvenient to be glancing over the shoulder continually, and then there is always a chance to secure game if one can watch ahead. The bow-facing rowing gear is also the proper thing for the duck hunter. The Lyman Gun Sight Corporation make bow-facing oar locks. Some parties attach a keel to the bottom of the boat and this makes it steadier but will not allow of use in shallow water. For the trap line, therefore, I advise the use of a boat having no keel.

A boat such as described will ride the water nicely, for being widest forward of the center, when the weight is evenly distributed it will set just a trifle deeper at the stern, allowing the bow to rise to the top of the water. The size will be about right to accommodate two men and if necessary will carry quite an outfit besides. But when taking a complete camping outfit, food, traps, etc., a larger boat will be more convenient.

Flat bottom boats with wide flaring ends are used considerably for fishing in still water. Almost everybody is familiar with that type and no description is necessary. They can be made by anybody who can use a saw, hammer and square.

CANOES. On the northern water courses there are three distinct types of canoes in use, namely, the all wood, the canvas and the Indian birch bark. The bark canoe can be procured only from the Indians, the others are manufactured and for sale by the various canoe makers of the North and East. There are many who suppose that the all wood canoe is not serviceable when used in rough water, but they really do stand considerable rough usage.

All canoes require care in handling, but there are times when no matter how careful the canoeman is, the rocks and snags will make their presence apparent by contact with the boat. The wood canoe is being used at present by Revillion Bros., who have trading posts through the Hudson Bay territory. I believe though that they have their canoes made with a narrow strip of wood over each seam.

The canvas canoes on the market are in reality made of wood and covered with filled and painted canvas, but the wood planking is very thin, only 1-8 or 3-16 inch. They are perhaps the most durable canoes made, as they are not easily punctured and are easily repaired by means of a piece of cloth, some white lead and varnish.

Some of the Northern Indians, now that good bark has become scarce and almost impossible to procure, have taken to making their canoes of canvas, working on the same principle as when making one of bark. To make a craft of this kind, proceed in the following manner:

MAKING A CANVAS CANOE. The ribs and lining are made in advance and allowed to become thoroughly dry. Ribs may be made of cedar, but balsam or black spruce are better, and when these woods cannot be had, any light, free-

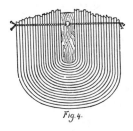

Fig. 4.

The Ribs on the Form.

bending wood will do. These ribs should be from ¼ to ⅜ inch in thickness, depending on the size and the desired weight of the canoe. They should be about 2 inches in width and must be split, shaved and planed to those dimensions. If sawed they will not stand bending.

After the ribs are made they should be thrown into water to prevent drying, and when a sufficient number have been made up they should be bent over two forms as shown in Fig. 4, and allowed to become thoroughly dry, which will require several weeks. It will be noted that those first placed on the forms will be the proper size and shape for use in the ends of the canoe, while those on the outside of the pack are right for the center. In putting the ribs into the canoe one works each way from the center, and this will necessitate two ribs of each size and shape, hence the two forms.

The lining is next prepared and allowed to become thoroughly dry. It is made up in strips of 2 or $2\frac{1}{2}$ inches in width, about 3-32 of an inch in thickness for an ordinary two man canoe, and of a good length, preferably the length of the proposed craft. Cedar is the wood usually selected for the lining.

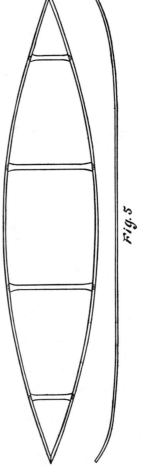

Fig. 5

The Gunwales Bent to Shape.

For the gunwhales, which are also made in advance, two long strips of tough wood will be required. It is best to split these from the tree and shave them down to a diameter of one inch each way, the corners rounded. For a 14 foot canoe, these gunwales should be 14 feet long. The curve will shorten them somewhat and trimming the ends into shape will also reduce their length some but it will be noted that the ends of the canoe curve and this will bring the length back to 14 feet. They should be steamed and bent as in Fig. 5, and allowed to dry on a form,

Length 14 feet 9 inches
Width 6 feet
Fig. 6.

The Shaped Canvas.

when the crossbars, four in number for a 14 foot craft, should be mortised into place as shown in the cut, and fastened with a few small nails. Such a sized craft should be three feet wide in the center. Therefore, the two center crossbars placed $3\frac{1}{2}$ feet apart should each be 2 feet 8 inches in length. The other two crossbars which are each placed two feet from the ends would measure about $16\frac{3}{4}$ inches each in length.

The next step is the cutting of the canvas, (12 oz. double filling duck) and if possible it should be made from one piece, the shape shown in Fig. 6. For a canoe of the size described, the canvas must be 6 feet wide and this will allow for two inches on each side, for folding and tacking to the gunwales. It should measure 14¾ feet in length to allow for the curve of the sides and good seams in ends. It is then fastened to the gunwales, on the outside, and tacked on the top edge with very small flat headed tacks, placed close together. Fasten the ends first, then the center, then midway between, etc., so as to eliminate folds and wrinkles. The ends of the canvas should then be sewn up, seams inside.

The strips used for the lining must be fastened together at each end, with a cord and hung in place inside of the canoe. These strips should fit up neatly, one against the other. The ribs are then put into place. These are trimmed to the required length, and starting at the center and working alternately towards either end, are sprung into place under the gunwales. To make a really strong canoe and to have the canvas stretched perfectly tight, put the ribs close against one another, but it is a common practice to leave a half inch space between each. The ribs stretch the canvas firmly and press the lining tightly against it. When finished, it will be stretched perfectly tight and smooth. Before placing the ribs in the ends a narrow half round strip should be bent to the proper shape and fitted in, covering the seam and stretching it to the proper shape. A thin narrow strip of wood is then nailed on the top of the gunwales to cover the edge of the canvas.

At no time during the construction of the craft must the canvas be allowed to become wet or even damp, for it shrinks when wet and cannot possibly be stretched to its fullest extent. Neither should it be wetted before use.

The last stage is the oiling and painting of the canoe. Boiled linseed oil should be used, and it should be heated and applied liberally when hot, and allowed to dry thoroughly before painting. Only the canvas, gunwales and cross-bars need be painted. Fig. 7 shows the finished canoe.

Such a canoe cannot be made in a day. It will require a week of careful and tedious work, but when finished will be a boat to be proud of, and, with care and an occasional coat of paint will last for years. For the inexperienced the making of a canoe of this kind will be difficult and it should only be attempted by those who are very careful workmen and experienced in the use of tools.

THE BIRCH BARK. A birch bark canoe is made in practically the same manner. The bark is sewn up with split and boiled spruce or tamarack roots, and this must be done while the bark is fresh from the tree. As it is slow work, several squaws will work together in the sewing, so that it may be finished before it becomes too dry. The bark is also sewn to the gunwhales, not nailed, and is placed with the "flesh side" out. To give it the proper shape, two sets of stakes are driven firmly into the ground and the ends of the canoe pinched between these stakes. The ends also rest on blocks of wood and the inside is weighted with stones to give the curve to the bottom. The seams are then daubed with boiled spruce gum, which hardens immediately on cooling and makes the canoe perfectly waterproof.

All of the bark canoes have the bottom more curved than that of the wood canoes and this is a decided advantage in rough water as it allows the craft to be more easily steered where quick turns are required. On the other hand, the straight

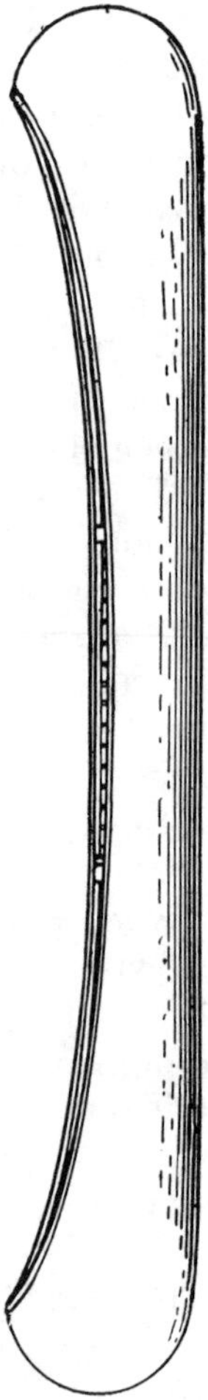

Fig. 7

The Finished Canoe.

bottom of the cedar or basswood canoe is better in still water, as it is steadier and not inclined to swing about at each stroke of the paddle. Many of the Indians make their canoes almost round on the bottom and such are always cranky and dangerous for the novice. The most satisfactory kinds have the bottoms slightly flattened. The ends should be of medium height. If too low the waves are likely to break in and if too high the craft is hard to manage in a wind.

We read that it is a rule among canoemen to have the paddle of the same length as the user.

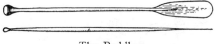

The Paddle.

Personally, I have never noted this, although there is no doubt that a tall man can use a longer paddle than a short one. The Indians, and all of the expert northern canoemen squat in the bottom of the canoe, sitting on their feet. Perhaps for that reason they are inclined to use shorter paddles than those furnished by canoe makers. Although I am a tall man myself, measuring 6 feet in height, I prefer a paddle only about 4 feet 10 inches in length. It should be made of light, strong wood, maple is commonly used, should balance perfectly and have a blade of medium width, quite sharp on the edges. Two paddles should go with each canoe, even if only one is used. A paddle is likely to be broken or lost at any time, and then too, they will both be needed when portaging.

The art of handling the paddle can only be

The Steering Stroke.

learned by experience, or by working in company with an expert. I will say, however, that one should learn to dip deep so that the entire blade is beneath the surface, to make a long, steady stroke and close to the side of the canoe. Learn to dip the paddle quietly, without a splash, and let each arm do its share of the work. The paddle is turned at the finish of each stroke and lifted edgewise from the water. When steering one should finish the stroke by giving a short lateral swing to the blade of the paddle. This will overcome the tendency of the canoe to move in a circle.

A canoe is usually manned by two persons; the one in the bow paddling straight along and the stern man steering. They paddle on opposite sides and as it is often desirable to change off one should learn to paddle and steer on either side. One man alone should sit in the center and should allow his paddle to run well to the rear before lifting it.

A canoe is a dangerous craft at the best and one should never forget where he is when using one of them. The beginner will be stiff and awkward and will try to keep the boat balanced. This is a mistake for the canoe will balance itself and he should allow it to move freely under him, letting it rock over the waves as it likes. The secret is in having a limber back and always keeping the body erect.

However, accidents are likely to happen no matter how expert one may become, and it is a wise precaution to attach one of the paddles to the crossbar by means of a cord some five or six feet in length. Then if the canoe should be capsized in a bad wind or rough water, one can at least regain the overturned craft and keep afloat. It is a good plan also, in rough water, to tie the most valuable goods, such as gun and food, to the crossbar, and then in case of an accident it would not go to the bottom anyway.

I have heard of one party of two men who, while attempting to run a dangerous rapid fully a hundred miles from civilization, had their canoe demolished and their entire outfit was lost. One man, after rescuing his companion managed, by swimming a mile down stream, to collect barely enough of the food to sustain life until they reached the railroad. This incident occurred in northern Ontario, and the two men were on a trading expedition. They lost a valuable outfit which had cost a considerable sum of money.

Canoes are usually managed with the paddle, but in ascending swift streams it will sometimes be necessary to use a push-pole, and this is quite an art in itself. A long light cord, or "tracking-line" is also used at times, to tow the craft along shore. If there are two in the party, the cord should be attached to the crossbar forward of the center and one man must stay in the canoe to steer. If there is only one man he must fasten the cord to the bow and wade the water.

When making extended trips into the northern forests, the canoe is often necessarily overloaded, and the gunwales are just a short distance above the water line. In such cases there is sure to be more or less water find its way into the craft, and the occupants should be supplied with a couple of large sponges with which to dry it occasionally. It will also be necessary to place a couple of small poles in the bottom, in order to keep the goods dry.

Canoes of all kinds are frail affairs, and require considerable care in handling, to guard against snagging. The most danger is along shore, and a good canoe is sometimes ruined by the novice, by stepping into it while one end is resting on the bank. The proper way is to turn the craft sidewise in water deep enough to float it easily, and drawing it up close to the shore, reach over the canoe with the paddle and support your weight partly on it while stepping in. Set the foot fair in the center and kneel down at once, or what is better, sit down on your feet.

For a while this position will be found to be extremely tiresome and the feet will go to sleep, or become cramped, but one will get used to it in a short time.

As before mentioned, the canoe is likely to be damaged on the snags, especially if it is a birch bark, and one should always be prepared to make repairs. For this purpose clean spruce gum is used, and one must have some vessel to melt it in. An enameled iron teacup, such as is used by campers, is good and much used for the purpose. The melted gum is smeared over the damaged place and hardens immediately. A large break may be mended by gumming a canvas patch over it. Old canoes are likely to leak at the seams and may be put into good shape by running over the bad spots with a hot iron.

The birch bark owes its popularity to the ease with which it may be repaired and to its light weight. I have seen a small canoe, capable of carrying two men, that weighed only twenty pounds, but the ordinary weight of the 12 or 14 foot craft is from thirty to fifty pounds.

Unless the ground is extremely rough one man can easily portage such a canoe a long distance. The proper way is to tie the paddles to the two center crossbars, and by turning the craft upside down one may allow the paddles to rest on his shoulders and steady the canoe with one hand.

Perhaps the finest birch bark canoes are made by the Montagnais of the Gulf of St. Lawrence. They are as well made as the finest cedar canoes turned out by the various manufacturers, and will cost about twenty or twenty-five dollars each. Those made farther west are comparatively rough and far less care is used in making them. They may be obtained for from six to ten dollars.

It will be noted that I have been speaking of the smaller craft such as is used by hunters and trappers. Some very large canoes are also made and used, those employed by the Hudson's Bay Co. being very large, capable of carrying a ton or more of freight and requiring six men to handle. Under favorable conditions they are sometimes rigged with a sail, but in order to use a sail with a bark canoe one must have a favorable wind, for there is neither keel nor lee-boards to prevent the craft from drifting sidewise.

MAKING A SAILBOAT. Sailboats usually have a rounded bottom but for ordinary use it is not necessary that it be so. While I could tell how to construct such a craft, it would be exceedingly difficult to tell it in an understandable manner and it follows that the construction of such a craft would be even far more difficult. But for use on our inland waters, especially for river use, a boat made on the same plan as the rowboat before described, will make a good practical boat and while the dimensions must be different the boat need not be large. For knocking about on the rivers and small lakes for pleasure, or for fishing, trapping, etc., a boat of the following dimensions will be found about right: Length over all 16 feet, width across gunwales at widest point, 4 ft. 6 in., bottom at widest part 3 feet, height of sides 18 inches, flare of side 9 inches, to be made of $\frac{1}{2}$ inch clear lumber, preferably pine or basswood, over 2 inch oak framework. To make such a boat, follow the instructions already given for rowboats, bearing in mind the difference in measurements. If desired, it may be decked over at the bow and stern, but this is not necessary for a river boat. It should have a keel such as shown in the diagram, 10 or 12 inches deep and must also have a rudder.

Presuming that the boat has been constructed as already described, make the keel as shown, cutting it from an oak board 1 inch in thickness and fasten it to the bottom by means of small iron brackets and wood screws. Be sure to set these brackets where the screws will strike the inside cross strips on the bottom.

The rudder should be made of oak, 12x18 inches. The shaft to which it is fastened is made of iron, forked at one end, spread and shipped over the board where it is fastened with screws. To accommodate this iron fixture a block of wood is fastened to the bottom of the boat, inside, and directly over the end of the keel. A hole of the proper size is then bored down through the block and bottom of the boat and a section of iron pipe inserted. The rudder shaft works in this pipe. The cracks around the block and iron pipe must be well closed against

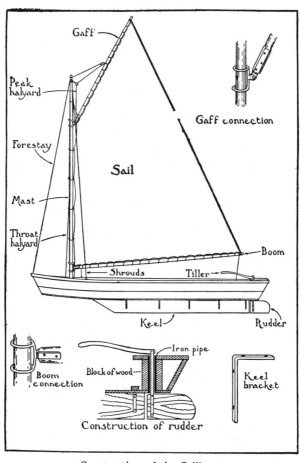

Construction of the Sailboat.

the ingress of water. Use white lead for this purpose. The tiller may be of iron or wood, as desired.

The mast is set well up in the bow. Fasten a piece of hardwood planking across the bow of the boat, fixing it securely to the gunwales and fasten a smaller block across the bottom, inside, and directly under the first one. This lower block should be 3 inches thick. Now make a $2\frac{3}{4}$ inch hole down through the upper plank, exactly in the center and another one in the lower plank, letting it down into the wood 2 inches or more. This constitutes the mast step.

The mast should measure 13 feet over all, $2\frac{1}{2}$ inches in diameter at base, 3 inches in the center and $1\frac{3}{4}$ inches at the top. The boom should be 11 feet long, inboard end 2 inches in diameter, center $2\frac{1}{2}$ inches, outboard end $1\frac{1}{2}$ inches. The gaff should measure 7 feet in length, inboard end $1\frac{1}{2}$ inches, center 2 inches and outboard end $1\frac{1}{4}$ inches in diameter. These spars and mast should be of some strong, light, straight grained wood. Spruce is the best but any good wood will answer.

The gaff has a folded strip of iron over the inboard end and is fixed with a small bolt to the sliding iron collar on the mast. This permits its being raised or lowered on the mast, hoisted at the peak, and swung around to either side to catch the wind to best advantage.

The boom is fixed solidly to the iron collar, so that there will be no trouble in stretching the sail and at the same time it may be swung around to either side desired.

The sail should be made of good 10 oz. duck. The dimensions are as follows: Hoist (inboard side) 7 ft. 10 in.; luff (outside edge) 15 feet, boom 11 feet, gaff 7 feet. The outside sail should be bound with codfish line or $\frac{3}{8}$ inch rope, the top and bottom sewn to the gaff and boom and the inboard edge should have rings of heavy telegraph wire inserted, they being made of such a size that they will travel easily on the mast or about $4\frac{1}{2}$ inches in diameter.

A system of tackle blocks for setting the sail may be arranged almost any way one desires so that the sail may be raised and stretched easily. The one shown is simple and effective and consists of only two blocks for rigging the peak halyard and one for the throat. They should be tied to the mast and gaff so that they will allow the sail to be swung around. To make the mast stiff and strong and reduce the strain on the boat one should stretch a forestay and shrouds from the top of the mast as shown in the drawing. Also attach a light rope to the outer end of the boom, with which to handle the sail and fasten it against the wind.

Hoist the sail and stretch it by hauling on the halyards, fastening same to some kind of fixtures near the foot of the mast. It may then be swung to either side as conditions require and the man at the helm has control of the sail with one hand while the other controls the rudder. The boat will run before the wind or directly across it, and because of the deep keel and flat bottom will not sidedrift much. When not in use the sail may be lowered and simply wrapped around the boom, the same lying lengthwise of the boat, where it will not be much in the way.

CHAPTER XI.

ITHOUT snowshoes, bush travel in winter would be impossible, throughout the greater portion of Canada, the most northern states, the mountain regions of the West and Alaska. As those portions of North America are the hunting grounds of the professional trapper, it will be seen that they are a very necessary item and without them he could do nothing in his line of work. Snowshoe tramps are also becoming more and more popular in the North, among all lovers of outdoor life, and each season adds a considerable number to the list of snowshoeing enthusiasts.

Just where, when and among what people the snowshoe originated, I am unable to say, but believe that they were first used by the American Indians, for the early explorers found them in use in all of the northern portions of this continent. At present they are also used in the northern parts of the "Old World," but there the ski is far more popular, and the web shoe is

135

only used when the snow is in a very loose condition or where the surface of the country is very rough and broken.

Necessity is the mother of invention, and it

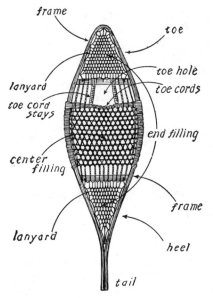

The Detail of a Snowshoe.

was necessity that led to the invention of the snowshoe. I have no doubt that the first snowshoes were crude affairs, for the early savages had no metal tools with which to fashion the frames or to cut the parchment for the filling. Perhaps too the first snowshoes were made entirely of wood, for it must have taken a considerable length of time to study out the intricate system of weaving that is now used. Anyway a system was adopted and practically all of the snowshoes now in use are made on the same general plan, even though the styles vary greatly in size, shape and detail.

In describing the various types, I will find it necessary to mention the different parts frequently, and that the terms used in designating these parts may be understood by those who are unacquainted with snowshoes I will give a diagram showing each part.

There is always an outer frame, rim or bow of light, tough wood, and it is bent in many patterns, but the most common style is that shown in the small cut. This frame is kept spread by two wooden braces placed, as a rule, about 16 inches apart, and mortised into the frame. This divides the shoe into three parts, the toe, center and heel. Small double sets of holes are drilled through the frame around the toe and heel, and into these holes is strung a slender strip of rawhide, called a lanyard, to which the filling is woven. The filling for the ends (heel and toe) is usually cut very light and strung close. In some sections seine twine is used instead of rawhide for filling the ends. The center is filled with heavier rawhide and the mesh is much coarser. Instead of having holes through the frame in the center to hold the filling, the

Snowshoeing.

strands are looped around the bow. This leaves the wood stronger and enables one to use heavier material for filling, and also gives the shoe more of a grip on the snow. Occasionally the centers are filled in the same way as the ends, but that style is not popular, as the shoes are very slippy when crossing logs.

To accommodate the toes of the wearer, there is a "toe hole," and just under the ball of the foot is the toe cord, a bunch of rawhide strands, and at this point the greatest strain comes on the filling. The toe cord is supported by the toe cord stays, which are several strands of rawhide, wound.

No matter what the style of the shoe may be, the method of attaching it to the foot is always the same, in principle. There is always a toe strap of some sort and the shoe always hinges to the foot at this point. Another strap passes around the foot above the heel to support the weight of the snowshoe when the foot is raised.

By noting the picture of the man on snowshoes it will be seen that the toe digs down through the toe hole when the foot is lifted, and in walking one-half of each shoe is lifted over the half of the other. The various styles of fastening will be described later.

In traveling about through the different parts of the country one can not help noticing the great difference in pattern of the snowshoes used, for they vary greatly in shape, from the round shoes of the Montagnais in Eastern Quebec to the long narrow upturned snowshoes of the

Various Styles of Snowshoes.

Crees in the Northwest. In the two plates shown herewith I have endeavored to show the various styles with which I am acquainted, and will describe each in detail.

The first (Fig. 1) is the regulation Eastern, or Algonquin style, made quite wide in proportion to its length. The length is about 38 inches and the width at widest part, 15 or 16 inches, toe round, hollowed somewhat on the sides, heel proportionately long and narrow. The frames are made of ash and the wood is worked out to a thickness of about ¾ inch at the heaviest part, nearly square, dressed down thinner at heel and toe. The heel is heavy and greatly outweighs the toe, making the shoe very nice for straight away walking, but bad for turning. The toe is slightly upturned, an advantage in loose snow but bad for hill climbing.

For thick brush it is supposed to be an advantage to have the shoe short, but this necessitates a greater width, and I cannot see that anything is gained by making the shoe short, except that it enables one to take a shorter step. In thick brush one can turn more easily with the short shoe, but the long narrow shoe is better for straight walking where the brush grows close.

Fig. 2 is the same shoe made longer and narrower. It is a more common type than Fig. 1, and is probably better for general use, in fact, it is one of the neatest and best shapes. In the one shown, single holes are drilled for the lanyard, which is held in place by looping around a bunch of wool yarn. This is no better than the other way, but the bright colored yarn adds to the attractiveness of the snowshoes, and this "tufted" style is much used by the northern Indians. Ladies' snowshoes are usually tufted. These two patterns, Fig. 1 and Fig. 2, are more generally used than any other, and are especially popular in the East.

Figure 3 is the Ojibway or Chippewa style, used almost exclusively by the Ojibway Indians and the white people of the same section. It is the only snowshoe I know of having a square toe. This is a decided advantage in hill climbing, as it takes a good grip on the snow. It is never upturned at the toe, and as a rule the toe is made broad so that it will cover a large surface.

The frame is made deep but is worked down quite thin at the ends. The average size is about 13x44 inches, and it is a good one for general use.

Figure 4 shows a style which is quite popular in Northern Michigan and parts of the New England States. The toe is round and very broad; the heel narrower. The object in proportioning a shoe like this is to cause the toe to stay near the surface of the snow, while the

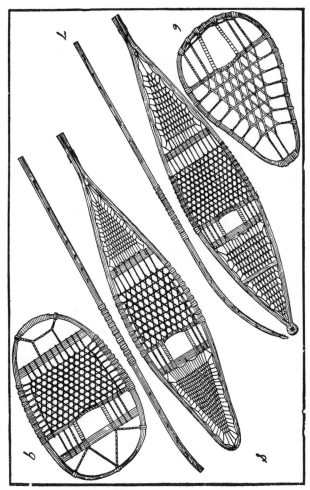

Other Styles of Snowshoes.

heel or tail cuts down. This makes the shoe lift easily when in deep loose snow, and is less fatiguing than the small toe kind. The toe cord is usually broad and flat.

The odd little shoe shown in Fig. 5 is a style used in the Adirondack Mountains of New York. As will be noted, the ends are not filled, and the center filling is usually cut very heavy and strung in with a wide open mesh. The forward cross brace is also shaped to accommodate the toe of the wearer. The toe is broad and the heel narrow.

It would appear to many that this style would not be satisfactory, and it probably would not be in the loose powdery snow of the far North, but in New York where the snow is usually of a "packy" nature or crusted, they are said to work nicely.

In figures 6, 7, 8 and 9 we have some extreme styles. Figure 6 is known as a "bear paw" snowshoe, and this name is given to all of the short, tailless styles. It is used mostly in the mountains of the Northwestern States. It is markedly different from all other styles in that it has no braces supporting the frame, but the filling is strung in such a way that it draws evenly from all points. The shoe is made somewhat rocker shaped, and this throws the filling up in the center, making the snowshoes springy to the step.

The frame of this shoe is usually made of a slender rod of service wood, left in its natural round state. The ends are lapped at the heel and firmly bound with rawhide. The bear paw shoe is the best style for use where the surface of the country is very rough and the snow heavy and "packy."

Number 7, which is known as the Cree pattern, is another extreme style. This shoe is used mainly by the Cree Indians of Northwestern Canada, but is also used considerably in other parts where the snow is deep and soft.

As shown in the cut, the snowshoe is long and narrow, the regular size of men's shoes usually measuring 5 feet in length by 12 inches in width. The frame is made in two pieces, joined at heel and toe, and the wood is usually worked out square, measuring about $\frac{3}{4}$ inch at the heaviest part, that is, in the center of the shoe. The toe is curved upward more than in any other style, being elevated sometimes as much as 8 inches. With this extreme curve it is necessary to have the toe of such a length that it will not strike the knee of the wearer when walking. In addition to the two cross bars there are one or two small ones across the toe to give the curved shape to the filling.

The Cree pattern snowshoe is a good one for fast travel in deep loose snow, or for use on smooth ground, like the prairie country of the far North. For use on a broken trail where the snow is hard or on the ice, it is not good, as it is slippy and likely to make the feet sore because of the upturned toe, which makes the frame very stiff. For easy walking a snowshoe must have a certain amount of spring, and this quality is lacking where the toe is curved, as it is in the Cree snowshoes. The curved toe is also bad for hill climbing.

Figure 8 shows a style which is very good for fast travel in loose deep snow, and for general use is far superior to the Cree. The length is about five feet or a few inches less and the width about 13 or 14 inches—toe slightly curved. For the trapper in the more northern sections a pair of snowshoes of this kind will be very useful for exploring country and prospecting for fur, or for breaking out fresh trails over the lines. He should also have another pair of the standard size and shape.

Number 9 is another "bear paw" snowshoe, quite popular in the New England States and the Adirondack Mountains. It is much used by the "spruce gummers," as the short oval style is best for sharp corners or for walking around trees, etc. I believe that it was originally designed by the gum hunters, and it is made by a number of Eastern manufacturers. The standard size is 16x26 inches.

The various shapes illustrated are modified in many ways, so that one seldom sees two pairs of shoes that are exactly alike. They are filled in more or less fancy designs, and the frames are changed slightly in shape, so that it is sometimes difficult to tell to just which pattern a snowshoe belongs.

Besides those described there is one more very marked pattern. I refer to the style used by the Indians of Alaska. It is of large size, being long in proportion, toe very broad, heel broad and with an extra brace or cross bar, toe slightly curved and the filling of the center strung in a wide, open, rectangular mesh.

When selecting a pair of snowshoes there are many things to be considered. A heavy man must have a larger snowshoe than a light man, and a tall person can use the larger sizes more readily than a short man. If the snow never gets very deep, or if it is usually quite solid, small shoes should be selected, especially if the ground is rough and covered with boulders, fallen trees, etc. Where the snow gets damp and packy the mesh should be more open and coarse to prevent the snow from packing under the foot. If there are many hills, the shoe should be of the flat style and the toe of good width. These and many other things should be remembered when buying snowshoes.

It is always best to have snowshoes made to order, for the stock snowshoe is never satisfactory. They are as a rule of cheap, flimsy construction, the frames of poor wood and the filling not fully stretched. As a result when they get damp the filling bags and the frames soon take on a rocker shape. Such shoes only last a short time, and although they cost less in the beginning are expensive in the end. A pair of good snowshoes will cost from $5.50 to $7.50, seldom less. If you do not feel like paying that sum, learn to make them yourself. While they will cost just as much in time and labor the average man can usually find plenty of time which would otherwise be unprofitably employed, and then he can see just what goes into the construction and can bring in all of the good points and eliminate the bad ones.

For general use, where one can afford only one pair of snowshoes, I would recommend selecting a shoe on the lines of the one shown in Figure 2. It should be of the flat shape; frames made of white ash, yellow birch or hickory and of clear straight grained wood without a flaw. The cross bars should fit neatly in the mortises and the frame should be fastened at the heel with a strip of rawhide strung through gimlet holes, not with wood screws or nails as such a fastening is likely to cause the wood to split when crossing logs, etc. For the average person a size of 14x48 inches is right.

The shoe should almost balance when suspended midway between the two braces; the tail or heel being just a couple of ounces heavier. The heel should be narrow and the toe broad. This will cause the heel to cut down into the snow while the toe stays on the surface. In lifting the foot the toe lifts easily and the heel is inclined to hang back, making a well balanced shoe trail as nicely as one having a heavy heel, and the walking will be much less tiring, while turning will be easier. This point is worth remembering.

When I first commenced to wear snowshoes I used the Indian made goods, with their comparatively heavy heel and small toe. I found them all right on a broken trail, but where I found it necessary to break a new trail the walking was exceedingly difficult. This was because the snowshoes cut down evenly at each end and the difficulty of extricating them at each step was fatiguing, especially when some 5 or 10 pounds of snow would fall on top. After getting advice from many sources and trying various patterns I learned where the trouble was and how to avoid it. After that I made my own shoes, shaping them as above described, and had no more trouble from that source. Those who are used to the regular pattern will find this style awkward in the start, but in the end I am sure they will say that they are the best by far.

For the filling, I recommend light cowhide for the center, and finely cut calf skin for the ends. Cow or calf skin will outwear any other kind of filling that I have ever tried, and is less likely to be burned in drying than deer skin. For second choice I would recommend caribou skin, and lastly moose skin. This latter, however, must be handled carefully, as it is certain to be injured if dried rapidly. Caribou, cow and calf are less susceptible to heat.

Some of the dealers in cataloguing their goods speak of their snowshoes as being filled with "caribou gut." By that they simply mean caribou skin.

I am told that the Indians of Hudson Bay, in the past, sometimes used beaver skins for snowshoe filling, claiming that it was superior to any other material. At present, beavers are worth too much to be used in this way. The Alaska Indians sometimes use bear skin as they say it will not stretch as much as the skin of other animals.

The center filling should be cut **fairly** heavy and woven in with an open mesh, about ¾ inch in size. The ends should be much finer. The filling should be strung in very tightly. Some makers use varnish on the filling, but I do not think it advisable.

A Snowshoe Trail.

See that the toe cords are heavy and strong, also be sure that they are smooth under foot or they will make the feet sore. If in a cold country the toe hole should be quite large so that one can find room for plenty of footwear. For regular everyday use, such a snow shoe is bound to give satisfaction.

When walking with snowshoes one is certain to make a broad heavy trail, and those who have never used them often ask: How can one possibly get through the brush with such things on their feet? In reply I will say that one can go almost anywhere on snowshoes. The small brush are, for the most part, buried under the deep snow, and the others can easily be avoided. The user always watches ahead and runs his trail through the more open places.

Always blaze the trail well if you are not certain that you will be along again before it will be buried under a fresh snowfall. This is especially necessary in the open country where the wind and the drifting snow will soon obliterate a snowshoe track. If the trail is blazed it may be followed easily even if no marks show on the snow. Going over the trail once on snowshoes makes a solid smooth bottom for the entire winter, and although a foot of snow may fall before one can get around again, the blazed trees show the way and the walking will be much easier on the trail.

Never jump off of stumps, rocks or logs, as the strain on the snowshoes is severe. Also be careful in crossing logs, etc., so that the end of the shoe does not rest on a solid object, or the frame may break. If not, it will soon take on a rocker shape. Dry them when damp, but always

place them far enough from the fire to prevent
injury to the filling. In the spring when the
snow commences to melt and the weather is
warm they may be dried out of doors. In summer hang them up with a wire so that the mice
cannot reach them, as those little rodents will
soon destroy the filling.

There are various methods of attaching the
snowshoes to the feet, and three of the best
styles of fastening are shown here. A. shows
the Ojibway style used almost exclusively
throughout Canada. A toe strap passes over the
ball of the foot and is passed in and out through
the mesh of the filling. By passing through a
half dozen holes on each side it will be held securely. A narrow, four foot strap is then dou-
bled and the center placed above the heel of the
foot, the ends passed under the toe cord at each
side of the toe hole, brought up on top of the
toes and crossed, one string passing over and one
under the toe strap as shown in the cut. The
ends are then looped around the straps at the
sides, as shown, and both tied together above
the heel.

The advantage of this tie is that the shoes
may be taken off and put on again with less
trouble than with any other fastening. A simple twist of the foot is all that is necessary for
removing it, and it may be again attached with-

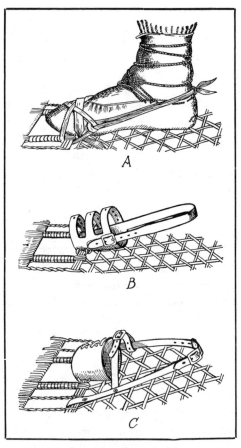

Snowshoe Fastenings.

154

out untying, a decided advantage in cold weather when one does not care to remove his gloves.

For strings, tanned caribou or moose hide, soft calf skin, lamp wick or folded and stitched cloth may be used. Very good strings may be cut from the tops of a pair of worn out shoes-pacs.

B and C are much used in the East. As they are plainly shown in the cut, no description is needed. They are less likely to make the feet sore than the Indian style, but they are not superior in any other way.

It is important that one use the proper footwear for snowshoeing. Leather shoes must never be used, as they will ruin the snowshoes and are too cold for winter wear. Wool lined overshoes, or arctics are not bad, but the snowshoes will not last as long as when using moccasins.

The Ojibway or Chippewa moccasins are best for use with snowshoes. They are soft and light, and when worn with plenty of heavy wool stockings are warm. I like the shape of the toe better than that of any other and the cloth top is more clinging than leather, holding the snowshoe strings in place, even though loosely tied. The Sioux pattern moccasins (the most common style) are likely to cause sore feet.

After a month or two of steady use snow-shoes will need repairs frequently. Always have a few strands of rawhide on hand and whenever a string breaks repair it at once. The very best shoes will stand just about one season of really hard tramping, such as the long line trapper does.

CHAPTER XII.

OW many woodsmen are able to make their own snowshoes? The number is comparatively few, but almost any person can learn if he is persevering and takes an interest in such work. There are very few white men who can weave the filling, and even among the Indians this work is done by the women, and perhaps not one buck out of a hundred knows how to do it. When he makes the wooden frames for the shoes and procures the parchment for the filling he considers his part of the work done, and turns it over to his better half.

If one can take a snowshoe and trace up the filling from the start he may learn how it is done, but this is almost impossible. Very few would even know where the strand starts in the weave. I believe that one can learn, however, by carefully following the directions which I am giving here, at the same time studying the cuts carefully. However, the frames must be made first.

The best woods are white ash, yellow and white birch and hickory. In the more southern districts it is possible that other equally good woods are to be found, but snowshoes are only used in the North, and the woods mentioned are the best, for the purpose, to be found there. In fact, throughout the greater portion of the northern forests the white birch is the only good wood to be found, and it is mostly with the working of that wood that I am acquainted.

The frames should be made in summer or early fall and allowed to become thoroughly dry before being filled, but I have known the Indians to make the frames in winter and fill them within a few days from the time of making.

Look along the edges of the swamps and you will find long slender birches with smooth bark. Select one of about six inches in diameter, free of knots and flaws for about ten feet. It should be straight and there must be no twist to the grain of the wood. If the limbs of the tree are drooping so much the better, as it is stronger wood. Avoid the red barked kind, with upright limbs.

Having found a good tree fell it, cut off about ten feet and lay this piece in a notch cut in an old log or stump. Now carefully cut a groove the entire length of the stick, making it an inch or more deep. Do not strike hard when cutting this groove, or you will shatter the wood. When finished, turn the stick over and make a similar groove in the opposite side.

Now go along the entire length and strike lightly with the axe in the bottom of the groove to start the split; turn the stick over and do the same with the other side.

Next make two small wooden wedges and commencing at the end of the stick, driving one wedge in each groove; keep moving them along and the stick will split nicely, following the grooves. If at any point the split is inclined to lead away from the groove, bring it back by cutting the contrary fibers.

Now select the best of the two pieces and cut another groove the entire length, on the bark side. Split this the same as before and you will have the wood for two frames.

In working the wood into shape the Indians use nothing but the axe and their strange curved knives, which are used for all kinds of woodworking. I have found it most convenient to use a rip-saw, plane and spoke-shave.

The bark side is always used for the outside of the frame and there should be very little taken off of it, except where it needs straightening, and at the toe, that is, the center of the stick, there should be nothing removed from the outside except the bark. Use care so as not to cut or fracture the wood on this side as it is likely to break in bending.

Ordinarily I work the stick down to a width of one and an eighth inches and the thickness varies from three-fourths of an inch in the center of the shoe (midway between the center and ends of the stick) to only a little over three-eighths of an inch at the toe (center of the stick), and less than five-eighths at the heel (ends of the stick). It must be a little more than twice the length of the proposed snowshoe. This would make a rather heavy shoe but the wood will shrink considerably in drying.

If you are not prepared to bend the wood at once, lay it in the water until such time. Put a kettle or other large vessel of water over the fire, and when it boils lay the stick across the kettle and mop it with the boiling water. A two foot stick with a bunch of rags tied on the end makes a good mop. Continue this treatment for fifteen or twenty minutes, then bend the stick over the knee, not too much, release it and bend again, working it back and forth to get it softened gradually. Then repeat the mopping and then the bending, increasing the bend of the stick each time. Only the toe, that is, the center of the stick need be steamed, but it is well to wrap a piece of cloth around the thickest part of the stick, on each side, and pour boiling water over occasionally while treating the middle. After about three-quarters of an hour of this treatment the wood will be so soft that it may be bent to shape.

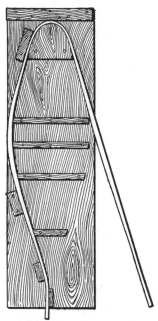

Bending the Frame on the Form.

Have a mould or form such as is shown in the cut, and a number of small blocks with nails already started in them. Place the wood on the form and bend slowly and steadily to shape, fastening by nailing the small wooden blocks against it. Both sides of the toe should be bent while it is still wet and hot, and before bending the other portions.

The other frame is treated in the same way and bent on a separate form. Be sure that they are both alike and that both sides of the frame bend evenly. When this is finished they should be set away to dry, which will require about a week. In bending the wood the outside of the toe is likely to splinter up some, but this can be dressed off afterwards. The cross bars should be made at the same time the frames are made so that they will become dry. When the frames are removed from the forms the cross bars should be mortised in. They should fit up as tightly as possible. It is well to leave the mortise a trifle small and after a few days fit the cross bar. In that way it is not so likely to become loose afterwards. The mortise should be one-fourth inch deep and the bar shaped as shown in Fig. 1.

It is very important that the cross bars be put in the proper place, for the balance of the shoe depends on that. Spring them in the frames about fifteen or sixteen inches apart and balance the shoe by suspending it on the hands, midway between the braces. Shift the braces until the heel is just a few ounces heavier than the toe, and they will then be in the proper place to mortise. I leave the tail quite long and make the heel end quite heavy. After the shoe is finished I cut it off to suit.

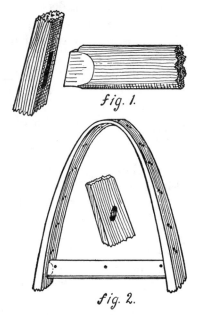

fig. 1.

fig. 2.

Mortise for Cross-bar, and Holes in Frame for Lanyard.

Fasten the ends of the frame at the heel by drilling two holes through and tying with a strip of rawhide. Countersink the string between the holes.

Fig. 2 shows the method of drilling the holes in the toe and heel, for the lanyard to which the filling is attached. They should be made with a one-eighth inch bit and the wood cut between about a sixteenth of an inch deep.

For general use, light cowhide makes the best filling for the center, that used in the ends should be lighter. Calf skin is best but seine twine is much used, and it is all right where the ground is not too rough.

The following is the way to prepare the filling: Take the green hide and stretch it well, allowing it to dry in that shape in a shady, airy place. Then with a sharp knife shave the hair off as closely as possible. Another way is to grain the skin while it is still green, which is done by scraping or shoving off the hair and scarf skin with a square edged instrument, the skin being placed over a beam. Perhaps this is the best way.

When it is desired to cut into strands the dry skin is dampened, all corners trimmed off and the cutting may be done with heavy shears or a small, very sharp knife. Follow the edge, cutting around and around, making the string widest where the skin is thin. The general width will depend on how heavy the skin is and how close you wish to weave the filling. When the strands are soaked and stretched, which is the next move, they will be considerably more narrow, and after being strung into the shoe and allowed to dry, they will be narrower still. The best way is to cut a few pieces beforehand, of

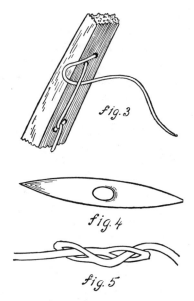

The Lanyard, the Needle, and Mode of Splicing the Strands.

various widths, soak them, stretch and dry. In that way you can tell just how wide to cut the thongs.

The lanyard is strung in the frame as shown

in Figure 3. It should be stretched very tight and allowed to dry before putting in the filling.

A needle will be needed for weaving and this is shown in Figure 4. It may be made of hard wood but is better if made of bone. It should be about two inches in length.

Figure 5 shows the mode of splicing the ends of the strings, for they will not hold if tied. I prefer to have them cut from eight to twelve feet long. When cutting, the ends should be left fairly heavy for some three or four inches, so that they may be trimmed off and a new eye made farther back if the splice comes in a bad place. A splice should never be made underfoot or on the frame.

To explain the various moves of the filling in an intelligible manner would be impossible, but I have made drawings which explain themselves. I always fill the toe first. In the drawing I have shown where the string starts and have numbered each round. Trace the filling carefully, the arrows show the course of the filling. It will be noted that in the toe every other round loops back around the one preceding it. The method of looping is shown in the small cut. This looping back throws the filling first to one side and then to the other.

Once the process of filling has gone so far as to reach the entire width of the end of the toe,

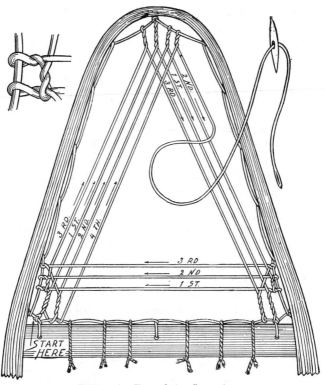

Filling the Toe of the Snowshoe.

the looping back is discontinued, and the filling is strung in the same as round number 3 until the toe is completed.

The rawhide strands must be soaked well and stretched before using, then soaked again and stretched into the shoe as tightly as possible. It is best to do the work over a tub of water, and if the strings are inclined to dry they should be moistened.

The filling of a section of the shoe must always be continued without intermission, until finished.

Be sure always to get every twist just right, and always cross the strings in the right way. I have gone to considerable trouble to show this clearly in the illustrations, and would advise that you keep them before you while doing the work. If a mistake is discovered, go back and correct it, even if you must remove half of the filling. During the process the mesh will get drawn out of shape some and it will be necessary to straighten it up occasionally. A one-half inch hardwood stick, whittled to a point, is good for straightening up the filling.

The filling of the heel is comparatively easy and is so plainly shown in the drawing that no description is needed. However, it is necessary that it be done just right, and I would advise

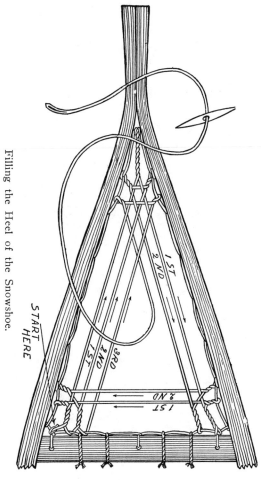

Filling the Heel of the Snowshoe.

169

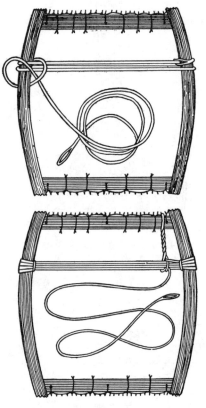

Putting the Toe-Cord in the Frame.

keeping the drawing in view while doing the work.

The center is more complicated and is filled on the same plan as the toe. The toe-cord or mainstay is put in first and this is plainly shown in the cuts. The string should cross the shoe four or six times to give it sufficient strength, for on this part comes the greatest strain.

Then the filling goes on as shown in the larger cut. Each round is numbered and the arrow shows the course. It should be noted that every other round loops back the same way as in filling the toe.

Here, instead of the filling twisting around a lanyard, it loops around the frame. The small cut shows how this loop is made. It is best if the edges of the wood are rounded slightly before filling. The Indians wind a strip of thin cloth around the wood, to prevent the filling from being cut by the sharp edges, but some people do not like this as they say the cloth holds the moisture so long that it causes the rawhide to rot.

The toe hole should be about four and a fourth or four and a half inches wide, and when only that much of an opening remains the filling should discontinue twisting around the forward cross bar and should only weave through the toe cord. Care should be taken to keep this portion

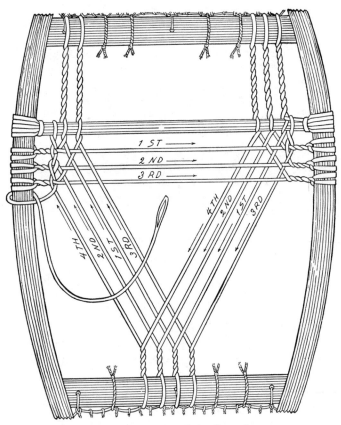

Filling the Center of the Snowshoe.

smooth as any knots or rough spots here will cause the wearer sore feet.

The filling will end in the very center of the toe cord and should be woven through here several times. After it is finished a strand of rawhide should be looped around the cross bar at the side of the toe hole and it should be passed

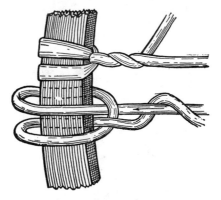

Mode of Looping the Strands Around the Frame.

down alongside of the toe cord support, around the toe cord, back and around the cross bar, then should wind closely about the entire bunch all the way down to the toe cord in and out through the cord to the other toe cord support, which should be strengthened and wound with the same string in the same way as the first. This gives additional strength and prevents wear on the most vital part of the filling.

When this is done, the snowshoe is finished and should be put away to dry. It should not be

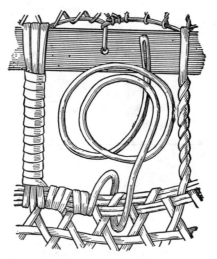

Finishing the Toe Hole.

exposed to the heat or the bright sunshine, but should be dried slowly.

Now I have described and illustrated as plainly as possible the common and most simple method of filling snowshoes. It may seem perplexing at first reading, but look over it again and study the cuts, then try to make a pair. You will find that it is more simple than it appears to be, and once you have filled a pair of snowshoes it will be easy afterwards.

After one has learned to make snowshoes such as described, he can by a little study, easily master the more intricate designs. Nearly all shoes are filled on the same general system, but each maker incorporates some little wrinkle of his own, so that one can seldom find two pairs of snowshoes which are filled exactly alike.

CHAPTER XIII.

IKE snowshoeing, ski (pronounced skee) running is becoming more and more popular each year as a winter sport. It is also the method of travel adopted by the trappers and rangers of many places in the Northern and Western United States and Canada, especially in those parts which have been settled by the people from Northern Europe. In Northern Minnesota and parts of New Ontario, which have been settled largely by Swedes and Finlanders the ski is quite common and is frequently seen.

Where the country is reasonably open and not too rough and the snow becomes fairly solid the ski is superior to the snowshoe, because one can travel far more rapidly than with the web shoe. However, in the dense woods where the brush grow close, the ground is covered with fallen trees and rocks, and the snow loose and powdery, the snowshoe is the only thing to use.

MAKING SKIS. Skis should be made of hardwood, white ash being probably best. But white ash is not to be had in the most northern parts of the country and birch (both white and yellow) and black or water ash is used. Although I am not certain I believe that hickory would be superior to all other woods. It is true that it is a heavy wood, but it is so strong that it could be worked down very light and it takes a very smooth finish, a necessary quality in ski wood.

Soft wood should not be used as it cannot be depended on for strength and there will be trouble from wet snow sticking to the skis, although red fir which is a western wood, is fairly good for this purpose, and is used quite often. Even the hardwood article must be "doped" to prevent this.

Turn to Chapter XII and read my instructions for splitting the wood for snowshoes. The wood for the skis should be split in the same way, by grooving both sides of the stick, but instead of splitting one half again, both halves must be used, one ski to be made from each piece, and a larger tree should be used, one about eight or ten inches in diameter.

Skis are made in varying lengths, depending on the nature of the country and the condition of the snow. In rough country where the snow is for the most part loose and fluffy, they should be about 7 or $7\frac{1}{2}$ feet long and $4\frac{1}{2}$ or 5 inches wide. For open smooth country, as on the plains, they are made from 8 to 10 feet long and four inches wide. The best size for general use is about 8 or $8\frac{1}{2}$ feet long and 4 inches wide. The weight of the user must also be considered, and those intended for use by a heavy man should be larger than those for a small man.

I give these measurements here that one may know how long to cut the wood. The half of the split piece should be fixed in a notch cut in the remaining piece of the tree, or any convenient log, and then hewn down on the flat side; the bark side should also be dressed down somewhat, but not much. This bark side is to be the bottom of the ski, and only enough should be taken off to give a 4 inch face to the stick. The stick should be dressed down to $1\frac{1}{4}$ inches with the axe, a little heavier where the toe strap is to be, and then the wood should be taken to a workbench or some place where a plane can be used.

The bottom should be planed smooth and one should see that it has a 4 inch face all along, then lay off one edge perfectly straight, make a line, and work the wood down to the line. Then with a marking gauge set at $4\frac{1}{4}$ inches, mark off and straighten the other edge. The extra $\frac{1}{4}$ inch is for shrinkage in drying.

Now measure and find the middle of the stick, and work it down here to a thickness of ¾ of an inch and taper it to ⅜ of an inch at 18 inches from the toe, from which point it should carry its thickness of ⅜ of an inch to the end.

Next measure back from where you commenced to taper the wood, about 11 inches, and from this point dress the wood down to about ¾ of an inch, tapering to ½ inch at the heel. The thick portion just back of the center should be about 1¼ inches thick. This is the part that comes under the foot of the wearer.

It is best to leave both ends of the ski a trifle longer than necessary, and then the ends may be cut off to make them balance at the toe strap, which is fastened at the forward end of the foot rest. Anyway they should balance from this point, and then when one wishes to go up a steep hill he can go sidewise, lifting first one foot and then the other. It-is also nice when you want to carry them in your hands, as they may be picked up by the toe straps.

Some ski users prefer to have the foot rest so far back that the toe will outweigh the heel, and then they weight the heel with lead to make the ski balance. They claim that when thus made the toe will be more certain to stay on the surface of the snow, but I believe that the majority of ski users prefer to have them as above.

The next move is to groove the bottom. This is to prevent the ski from slipping sidewise. A half round plane or gouge should be used and a $\frac{1}{2}$ inch groove should be made in the center, starting where the bend of the toe commences (about 18 inches from the point) and running to the end of the heel. It should be very shallow at the toe end and should run quite deep at the heel.

If it is necessary to make the heel lighter to cause the ski to balance, work some off on the upper side, starting in the center and beveling towards the edge. If necessary to make the heel heavier, drill some small holes in the end and pour in some melted lead. There should not be very much taken off the heel at one time, as the object is to have the heel stiff and the toe springy.

The best way to soften the wood for bending the toes is to mop them in boiling water as advised for bending snowshoe frames, bending them over the knee occasionally until they are thoroughly softened.

Take two fair sized sawed sticks about 6 or 8 feet long and nail a half round block between them at one end. Now nail two short pieces of the same material as used for the 6 foot sticks between them, one just forward of the center and the other one at the back end. They should be the same length as the half round block and should be spiked securely inside of the strips.

Near the outside of the half round block nail a small strip of wood, having a $\frac{1}{2}$ inch hollow on the under side. This will be better understood by viewing the illustrations.

This form must be made before the skis are ready for bending and when they are thoroughly soaked and softened by the boiling water, place the ends under the small strip on the half round block, side by side, and bend carefully until they touch the two cross pieces; then turn the form over on the floor and its weight will hold the ski in position; if not, it should be weighted. It should be remembered that they are to be given more bend than the finished ski is to have, as they will spring out somewhat straighter when released, no matter how dry the wood is. They should remain on the forms a week at least, for if removed too soon the bend is likely to spring out of the toe.

The Norwegian ski has a decided upward curve to the center. This makes it springy and the curved shape is much liked. This pattern is also made a trifle wider at the heel than in the center and the toe is considerable wider. This makes it ride on the surface of the snow very nicely.

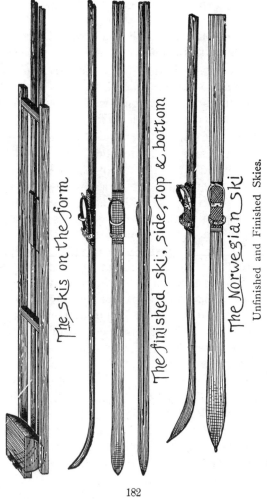

The skis on the form

The finished ski, side, top & bottom

The Norwegian Ski

Unfinished and Finished Skies.

When the skis are perfectly dry remove them from the form and apply hot pine tar to both top and bottom. Bring the tar to a boiling point and heat the skis by the side of the fire. Make them almost scorching hot and then apply the tar, allowing it to cook into the wood. The surplus may be wiped off and the skis allowed to cool. When the tar has hardened the wood will have a very smooth surface, making the skis very lively and easy running and preventing the wet snow from sticking to them.

All of the various methods of fastening are good. Perhaps the Norwegian pattern shown in the cut is best. In all cases there must be an adjustable toe strap. It is commonly attached to the sides of the footrest by means of nails, the leather being countersunk to prevent wear, but a far more satisfactory way is to make a slot entirely through the footrest and pass the strap through. There must also be an adjustable strap to pass around the foot above the heel, and it is best to have this strap attached to the edges of the footrest at about the center. It is, however, frequently fastened to the toe strap, but this arrangement, in my opinion, gives too much freedom of motion to the ski, and one does not have so much control of it.

It is best to tack a sheet of rubber to the top of the footrest, to give one's feet a good grip, but there are many who do not do so, preferring to wrap some sort of coarse cloth about the feet, such as burlap, or a torn-up gunny sack. Either way will answer.

The method of locomotion when using skis is a sort of skating movement. The ski pole is often useful. It is a light pole of about seven feet in length, having a sort of wheel on one end, and is used for pushing and as a support in going up steep places.

There is not likely to be any trouble from damp snow when skis are treated with pine tar, but if there is they may be given a second treatment when needed. There is a possibility of the surface wearing off when using them on a crusted snow, and this would necessitate a second application.

Another good preparation which is used in the same way, is the following: Three parts rosin, two parts beeswax and one part mutton or beef tallow. Mix and melt them together and apply in the same way as the tar. Either snow-shoes or skis are necessary to all persons employed out of doors in the North during the winter months.

TOBOGGANS. The bush toboggan must not be confounded with the same article which is used for coasting. It is somewhat different and serves an entirely different purpose. The trapper finds it very useful when moving camp, when setting out a long line of traps in winter or spring, when camping out for any reason, or when hunting for big game, for the bush toboggan is used as a means of conveyance and not for sport, or rather, it is not intended for coasting.

A toboggan may be used with a dog team or it may be drawn by hand. Small ones for use on rough trails or on the trap line may be made without much trouble.

Select a nice white birch tree about 15 inches in diameter, fell it and cut off a section, about 7½ feet long. Split it through the center by grooving it on both sides and then hew an inch board from each half of the log. Get the board from as near the bark as possible, for that is the toughest wood. See also that there are no flaws or streaks of red heart-wood.

The toboggan should be 14 inches wide, and this will require two boards having a 7-inch face. Another inch must be added to each to allow for straightening and fitting, and one-half inch for shrinkage. In other words, the rough axe hewn board must be 8½ inches wide and 7½ feet long by 1 inch in thickness.

Next, plane the boards perfectly smooth on the bark side. This is to be the bottom of the toboggan. Then straighten the edges and dress the other side down to a thickness of $\frac{3}{8}$ inch. The ends of the boards which are to be bent for the hood of the toboggan may be planed down to $\frac{1}{4}$ of an inch in thickness.

When the boards are finished, if you are not ready to bend them place them in the water until that time. The wood is softened by mopping with boiling water, the same as the skis and snowshoe frames, but as they must stand a hard bend, one should have them very soft before the actual bending process begins.

Provide a frame such as shown in the illustration and clamp the boards to it, have a roller such as shown and when the boards are ready to bend, slip the roller on the end and bend slowly and carefully until it has the desired curve, then tie the handles of the roller to the frame.

The cross bars should be made of good strong wood. They must be 14 inches long and may be either half round or square shape, about $1\frac{1}{4}$ inches in diameter.

On the flat side, or the side which is to go next to the boards, and an inch from each end, make a groove one-half inch deep.

When the boards are thoroughly dry so that there is no danger that they will lose their shape, the cross bars may be fitted on. There should be four of them for a toboggan of this length, and they should be placed an even distance

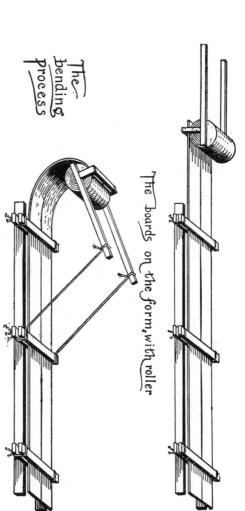

The bending process

The boards on the form, with roller

Construction of the Toboggan.

187

apart. They should be fastened by means of 1¼ inch wood screws, inserted from the under side of the toboggan, and the heads countersunk. The Indians bind them on with rawhide (baa-beesh), countersinking the strands between the holes, but the screws are best.

Fasten two small half round sticks, one on each side, to the end of the hood or curved part. The usual way is to drill a number of small holes through the boards, an inch from the ends, and tie the sticks with rawhide, "sewing" through the holes. Then from each end of these sticks fasten a piece of stout wire to the forward cross bar. This is to prevent the hood from losing its shape. The Indians sometimes use spruce roots for this purpose and sometimes cord.

Now take a piece of codfish line and tie it along the ends of the cross bars, stretching it thoroughly. Pass it through the groove on the under side of the cross bars, then up and under itself and on to the next cross bar.

Instead of a cord some use a straight stick about an inch in diameter and bind it along the side of the toboggan, on top of the cross bars. No matter which is used its purpose is the same, namely, to furnish a means of fastening the load to the toboggan. If sticks are used they should each project about two inches beyond the rear cross bar, which should be placed that far from the ends of the boards.

In the curve of the hood a few gimlet holes should be made, an equal number in each board, and about 1 inch from the inside edges. Through these holes run a piece of rawhide to hold the boards together, or sew them with spruce or tamarack roots.

A toboggan of this size is intended to be drawn by a man, and for drawing it a "tump line" or pack-strap is commonly used, but a light rope will answer. It is attached to the ends of the forward cross bar and a pair of stout screw-eyes furnish the most convenient method of attaching.

The bottom of the toboggan must be sandpapered and made as smooth as possible. They are seldom given any treatment to prevent the snow from sticking, but the pine tar treatment recommended for skis is good and it will make the wood wear better. It will not take long for the sharp crust of the spring snow to cut through the wood where the curve of the hood begins.

A toboggan can only be used on a smooth well beaten trail. The Indians, when setting out a long line of traps, proceed as follows: They first break a smooth trail, avoiding hills and rough ground wherever possible. A small wooden shovel is used to level the track along the sides

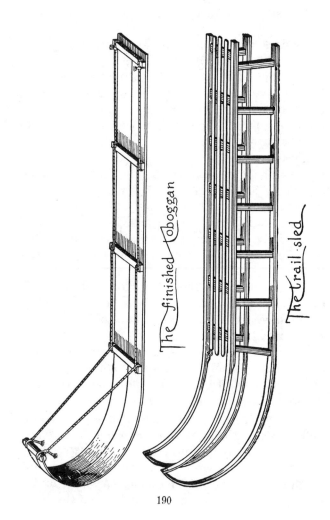

The finished toboggan

The trail-sled

190

of hills and on rough ground.   After the trail
has been broken a sufficient distance from camp
the trapper sets out with his camp outfit and
toboggan, camping at the end of the broken path,
from which point the trail is extended again,
and in this way he can run a longer line of traps
than when carrying his outfit on his back.

The Indians sometimes draw the toboggan
by passing the strap over the head, but the usual
way is by passing the strap or rope across the
back of the shoulders and under the arms.   The
rope should be held firmly with the hands to
relieve the shoulders from the strain.

In loading, a sheet of canvas is first spread
on the toboggan and the goods piled evenly the
entire length.   The edges of the canvas are then
folded neatly over and the load is bound securely
with a strong cord (codfish line), which passes
over the load and under the rope at the sides of
the toboggan, crossing back and forth the entire
length.

When camping for the night, do not let the
toboggan stand in the snow but turn it on its side
and brush all snow from the bottom or it will
freeze there and cause trouble.

The dog team toboggan is usually much
larger, sometimes 10 feet long and 2 feet wide.
The northern Indians make these with high fancy
shaped hoods.   They find the flat bottomed tobog-

gan better for the soft trails of the bush than the trail sled, which is used in the far North, and also on hard trails or ice in the timbered country.

TRAIL SLEDS. Trail sleds are light and strong, being made on the same plan as the child's coasting sled. They have broad high curved runners and slatted top. They are used in the same way as the dog toboggan. They are used in the barren grounds, but in the bush can only be used on a hard trail.

As used throughout the wooded portions of Canada, a dog team consists of from 5 to 7 dogs hitched single file. In some parts of the country farther north, larger numbers are used, and they are hitched on opposite sides of a single long trace. In the barren lands of the far North and the coast of Labrador they are hitched side by side each with a single and separate trace. But for the narrow snowshoe trails of the bush lands the only way is to hitch them single file, the traces of the leader attached to those of the next in order, and so on. Dog harness is always the simplest kind anyway. Breast collars are seldom used as the dogs can pull more when using a real collar. Trail dogs are trained for the work and the leader especially must be well trained. "Huskies" are used generally, but any intelligent dog may be broken to harness, and

when there is a rush into the frozen regions, for
any purpose whatever, all kinds of strong dogs
are bought up and broken for trail use.   The
"huskie" is too heavy for use on the soft trails
of the bush and the Indians use smaller dogs
for this purpose, the "Indian dogs" as they are
called.

CHAPTER XIV.

NDER this heading it would be possible to give quite a lengthy article, for there is much to talk about if one desires to cover the subject thoroughly, but this work is not intended so much for the sportsman or occasional camper, as for real followers of the trail, and for them the plainer and simpler style is most desired. For that reason I will tell only of the foods and the style of cooking that I have found good. There may be many better ways, and I will not feel in the least offended if you do not like my style, for really my own cooking has given me indigestion more than once. But I know from experience that it will answer under compulsory conditions.

CHOICE OF FOODS. The choosing of proper food for a lengthy trip into the woods or other place removed from civilization is an important matter and worthy of some study. One should choose such foods as give the maximum amount of nourishment and the minimum of weight and bulk. It should also be something which may be cooked very simply and be easily digested.

If one is going into a game country he can depend to a certain extent on fresh meat and in the summer on fish, but before doing so he should be certain that the game and fish are found there in reasonable abundance and that there is nothing to interfere with procuring it.

Except for very short trips, or where one will have an easy means of conveyance, such heavy and bulky goods as potatoes and other vegetables, canned goods and any other food which is very bulky or heavy or likely to freeze during cold weather must be omitted. In cold weather one may take onions for they are not harmed by freezing if they are not allowed to thaw again until ready to cook. For me, however, onions are indigestible. Potatoes will be missed some, but one can learn to do without them. There are dried potatoes on the market which are not bad when stewed but I cannot digest them.

The following list of a month's supplies for one man will show the kinds of food usually selected by the writer, and will make a good basis on which to figure for a long trip:

25 lbs. flour; 10 lbs. cornmeal; 1½ lbs. good baking powder; 3 lbs. salt; 10 lbs. bacon; 1 lb.

lard; 2 to 3 lbs. butter; 12 lbs. beans; 4 lbs. split peas; 5 lbs. evaporated fruit (apples, apricots or peaches) ; 4 lbs. prunes; 5 lbs. sugar; 2 lbs. tea; 1 tin of black pepper; a quart tin of maple or other syrup and a bottle of pickles. A few cans of condensed milk may be taken if you like it.

This may seem like a lot of food, but bush life develops a great appetite. If one is certain he will get plenty of game he may shorten the list somewhat but not much.

If one must do much back-packing, overland, it is best to have the flour in bags of a size that may be handled easily. The fifty pound bags will be heavy enough for most people. If you do not like cornmeal a little more flour may be substituted. Salt pork may be taken instead of bacon, if one prefers it. I like salt pork to cook with beans, and if going for a few weeks or longer I take both. Beans are very nourishing, perhaps more so than any other food. The split peas are excellent for soup and should not be omitted. Of dried fruits I prefer apricots and peaches, as apples are indigestible with me. One has a remarkable craving for sweets when in the woods but the syrup and sugar will satisfy it.

Many people prefer coffee to tea, but I have used both and will stand by the good grade of black Ceylon or India tea. It is the beverage of the Canadian bushman, Indian and white, and for strengthening and refreshing one when tired is superior to coffee or any other drink which I have ever tried. I drink it without sugar and always make it strong. Intoxicating drinks should never be taken into the woods when serious work is in prospect.

COOKING. It is in making bread that the amateur is most likely to fall down. In permanent camps where one may be home every night "sour dough" bread is very nice, but it needs considerable more care in making than baking powder bread. It is made by mixing a batter of flour and warm water, a very little salt and a spoonful of sugar. Let it stand in a fairly warm place until it ferments and lifts the cover from the pail, then mix in flour until you have a good stiff dough. Knead it well, and mix with it a teaspoonful of lard and one of soda. Then knead again and roll out to about an inch in thickness and it is ready for baking.

As this requires too much care for practical out of door men, I advise making baking powder bread. To a pint of flour add one teaspoonful of good baking powder and half that amount of salt. Mix it well and then add a lump of lard or bacon grease the size of a walnut. Work this well through the flour and then pour in enough cold water to make a thick but rather smeary dough. Mix it as quickly as possible but do not knead it.

Have the pan warm; sprinkle in a little flour; place the dough in it and spread it smooth and to a uniform thickness (about ¾ inch) with the back of the spoon, and bake it, first on one side then turn it and bake until done on the other side. Practice makes perfect. The one thing to remember is that the baking powder commences to act as soon as the water is added. It will be seen then that it should not be worked with more than necessary and should be put to bake as

Baking Out of Doors.

quickly as possible, for the baking powder will only act once.

It is presumed that this baking will be done in a permanent camp where one has a stove. If there is an oven the bread need not be turned, otherwise it must be baked on top of the stove, in the frying pan. Often when one side is baked I have stood the pan on edge by the side of the stove and allowed the baking to proceed in that way.

Out of doors another method is needed.   I have used the ordinary frying pan in the following way: Lay two green chunks or two square edged stones, about 7 or 8 inches apart, near the camp fire. Rake a few coals between and place the pan over them. Put the dough in the pan (after sprinkling with flour) and cover it with a sheet of tin. Place live coals on this cover, about twice as many as in under and watch the baking closely so that the bread will not burn. It will require only about 15 minutes to bake.

When camping out I seldom carry bread with me but carry the flour, already prepared, and make bread when I camp for the night.   In such cases I frequently omit the lard from the dough and simply turn the dough into the greasy pan after frying the bacon. I have bacon almost every meal when camping out on the trail.

A very nice article when in camp is the old standby, the pancake. Take a good handful of flour and a small one of cornmeal; add a half teaspoonful of baking powder, one of sugar and a little salt. Mix well, stir in water to make a thick batter, place with a spoon in a hot greased pan, and bake quickly. When small air bubbles show on top, turn and bake the other side. They are great with maple syrup.

As before stated, beans are one of the most substantial foods, but in order to have them nutritious one must cook them in the right way. They may be baked nicely in the following way:

Pick over about a pint of small beans, rejecting all imperfect ones (if it has not been done before going into camp) and wash them well, then put them to soak in cold water. Do this at night before going to bed and in the morning boil them until they crack open. Then have your kettle full of water and put a couple of slices of salt pork on top of the beans, add a spoonful of sugar and they are ready for baking.

Dig a hole in a dry place and put the kettle in it, covered with the frying pan. Throw about a shovelful of hot coals over it and cover it airtight with dry sods and ground. You can let this go all day and the beans will be nicely cooked in the evening.

In a permanent camp a bean hole may be made just in front of the fire place and lined with stones, so that it will be good at all times of the year and in all kinds of weather.

Properly boiled beans are in every way equal to baked beans, but comparatively few know how to cook them so that they are really good. In my opinion my way of cooking them is one of the very best. Wash and soak them the same as before mentioned and put them to boil with a piece of salt pork and allow them to boil (simmer) very slowly for two hours. By that time they will be cooked fine and the water should be allowed to get very low. If the salt from the pork is not sufficient seasoning, add some more, stirring well afterwards.

If you don't eat them all at the first meal you can warm them up and they will be better than before. Grease the bottom of the pan and turn them in, leave them bake until a light brown crust commences to form on the bottom then stir them so that they get browned on top.

Everybody knows how to fry bacon and nearly every woodsman knows how to fry steak. For those who do not know, I will give my method—there may be worse ways. Always cut the steak across the grain. Do not salt it. Use plenty of grease and have the pan smoking hot. Let the meat sear on one side then turn it. This closes the pores and prevents the juices from escaping. When fried on one side turn it over and salt it. If you like it rare, fry rapidly, otherwise give it plenty of time and do not have the pan extremely hot after the first turning. Many people like to fry onions with steak and it is all right if you eat onions.

In boiling meat it should be put on in hot water, unless it is intended for soup or stew, or you wish to use the liquor afterwards. In such cases it is best to put it on in cold water and let it come to a boil. Cook slowly.

In the woods, many odd dishes are compounded. For instance the following: After the meat has been boiled to a finish, remove it, leaving the small particles and stir into the boiling liquor a composition of cornmeal and flour, about two parts meal. Season with salt and pepper, using plenty of the latter and stir occasionally, to prevent it from burning fast to the bottom of the kettle. Let it cook slowly until thick, and eat it as soon as it is cool enough. If there is any left over let it get cold and slice it a half inch thick and fry in bacon fat. Try this one.

Good soups and stews may be made occasionally if one likes them; for my part there are a few to which I am partial. Pea soup is my favorite, and I make it by stewing small squares of salt pork with split peas. The pork must be partly cooked first, for the peas will be broken up and "mushy" after an hour's cooking. It must be boiled slowly and stirred frequently or the peas will burn fast to the bottom of the vessel.

I sometimes make a soup by boiling a handful of beans or barley with venison. The large narrow bones are best for soups, and they should be broken first. A soup made of the tail (with part of the back bone) of the beaver is about the best on the list, but there are very few woodsmen who can have it.

Small game birds and animals such as partridges and rabbits make excellent stews. Put them on in cold water and bring to a boil, allowing them to cook about twenty minutes, then pour off the water and put on fresh. Add a couple slices of bacon cut into little squares, an onion if you like it, a little butter if you have it to spare, some salt and plenty of pepper. Cook it slowly for two or three hours or until the meat is well done and partly off the bones, then brown lightly a little flour in the frying pan and stir it into the stew. Do not use much flour and don't give it too much color in browning.

Fish may be cooked in various ways. The best way I have ever found is to drop them in well seasoned, boiling bacon grease and cook them just the same way as doughnuts.

Both fish and game birds may be cooked by wrapping in green leaves or grass and burying in hot ashes and live coals. It is all right if done well but to be used only when necessary. A chunk of meat may also be roasted by tying up in a piece of the green hide of the animal and placing in the fire.

I do not consider it necessary to speak of cooking evaporated fruits, etc. Everybody knows how to do that.

This is my way to make tea. I bring the water to a boil then drop in the tea, remove the pail from the fire and cover it. The tea is well drawn in about five minutes. One thing which I would like to know, is how to make good tea from melted snow. I have tried it hundreds of times when there was no water to be had and could never make good tea in that way; it always has a rotten taste. I have tried everything I could hear of or think of but it was just the same. I have drank good tea made by others from melted snow but could not make it myself. I have watched the Indians make it and tried the same way without success.

One of my friends advises the following method which, up to date, I have not had the opportunity to try out.

"Have the tea pail clean, then fill it with snow. Rake a pile of live coals to one side of the fire and place the pail over them. When the snow is melted fill it up again and when this melts you have that much pure water with which to make the tea. Tea so made will have no bad taste. I think your trouble is caused by the fact (supposed) that you are always in a hurry and melt the snow too fast".

These methods of cooking and the kinds of food recommended may not meet the approval of many outdoor people, and if so I can only request that you do not jump on me too hard, for they are the best I know of and are from my own experience.

CHAPTER XV.

BUSH TRAVEL.

FTEN when I talk of my woods life my friends remark that they would not know how to travel in the forest. "Don't you get lost sometimes?" they ask. Now anybody may lose their bearings on a bad day, but no person with a knowledge of forest life should really become lost. To guard against it, learn to travel by direction,—North, East, South and West—and then remember you are east or west, north or south of the railroad, the lake, the river or the mountain. If you can do that you will never be badly lost, but you may for a while lose your camp, your trail, or even your hunting grounds. To travel by direction is better than to go by landmarks, for north is always north, but two landmarks may look exactly alike; then too, one does not know the landmarks when on strange ground.

On my hunting grounds I combine the two methods, and when I am not certain I go by direction. When locating in new territory I travel entirely by compass, or the sun, until I learn the "lay of the land." In other words, learn the locations of the principal streams, lakes and mountains. After one trip across country one can remember certain hills, tall trees, lakes and streams which will enable him to easily go over the same route again. Then when he sees these landmarks from other sides and learns their directions and distances from one to another, he can safely travel by landmark, but I always carry a compass when in the woods for one is likely to wander off into strange territory at any time, then too, the weather may turn foggy so that the marks cannot be distinguished, or they may be obscured by a rain or snow storm. Therefore, the compass should always be taken with you.

It is true that one may travel with fair accuracy by taking his directions from the sun, but as a rule when one cannot see landmarks he cannot see the sun either. I remember of one time when I was trapping in Canada that I had been using a small compass mounted in a square wood case. There was no way to fasten it to my person and I carried it loose in my pocket. Of course I lost it and for quite a long time I traveled without one, keeping my directions by the sun. It was late in winter and one of those dark, cloudy days, which are common at that time, and

I wanted to run a line of traps south from one of my little shelter-camps. Everything went well for quite a ways, and I set several traps for marten and fisher. After a while I saw a snow-shoe trail ahead of me. I thought of Indian trappers, and hurried to examine the trail which was made by Indian snowshoes, beyond a doubt. I stepped into the trail and found that my own shoes fitted exactly; then I realized that I had been walking in a circle and that this was my own trail.

Well, I got straightened out again and traveled on. Occasionally only I could get a glimpse of a bright spot in the sky, which showed me the location of the sun, but it would vanish again and leave me to wander on by guess. I set a few traps and after a while, knowing that the day was rapidly drawing to an end, I knew I must return to camp. I was near the top of an elevation, and a little draw leading diagonally down the side made a good place to set my last trap. I set it and then returned to camp over my broken trail.

A few days after I went to look at the traps. It was the same kind of a day, but this time I had the broken snowshoe trail to follow. When I reached the last trap I hurried on to see what lay on the other side of the hill. Imagine my surprise, when on reaching the top, I saw only a short distance below the small lake on the opposite side of which my camp was located. On my first trip I had traveled in a circle and set a trap within a mile of camp, thinking that I was far from my regular line, and then had walked back on that long trail when I could have reached camp in just a little while by going over the hill. This will show what one is up against when he tries to travel in the woods without a compass.

The Indians do not carry compasses, but they never venture far alone in strange country. If they do they go by directions given by some other person who has been over the ground. The sun is the Indian's compass and clock, it tells him which is north and south, and also tells the time of day accurately enough for his needs. On bad days he knows enough to stay in camp, and if, when travelling, he does not find a certain stream where he thought it was, he is not alarmed. He makes his camp at nightfall and next day continues his journey in the same direction until the stream is reached. The average white man would have changed his course when he thought he had gone far enough, and the chances are that he would have been lost. The Indian would consider it disgraceful to carry a compass, but on rare occasions even he gets lost.

As before stated, I always carry a compass

and I prefer a small one, open face style, with a ring so that it may be attached to my clothing by means of a strap. Usually I carry it in the pocket of my shirt, secured by a six inch strap. There it is easily reached when needed, is always with me and is not likely to be damaged when gathering the night's fire-wood, which it is likely

The Common Pocket Compass — A Favorite Style.

to be if carried at the belt. I never carry an ex-pensive compass. One costing a dollar is accurate enough for use in the woods, and when the needle post becomes worn so that the needle does not swing freely, I buy a new one and throw the old one aside.

In my opinion a needle stop is not a desirable feature in a woodman's compass, unless the case may be closed securely against the ingress of dust. As before stated, I prefer an open face compass, and the stop opening allows dust to enter, which makes the compass work badly. Of course, if the needle swings freely, the post will become blunted in time, but a dollar compass after a year's faithful service may well be thrown away and one can easily afford a new one.

All people living in or going into the wilderness know what a pocket compass is, and also how to use one, but there are many people, trappers and hunters at that, living in thickly settled parts of the country, who do not know what it is or how to use it. One party who was looking at my compass one time remarked "As I understand it one must know which is north before he can use the compass."

To those who do not understand it I will say that the blue end of the needle when allowed to swing free always points to the North, or near enough to the true north for practical purposes. Northwest of Hudson Bay is a point known as the Magnetic North Pole, and this pole attracts the blue end of the needle from all parts of the world, causing it to point in that direction. To be more accurate I believe that it really does not attract the blue end, but that it repels the other part of the needle, but be that as it may, the blue end points to this Magnetic Pole and we commonly say that the blue end points north. When the needle swings free and eventually comes to a stop, the compass may be turned easily until the letter "N" is under the blue end of the needle and then you have all points of the compass, North, East, South and

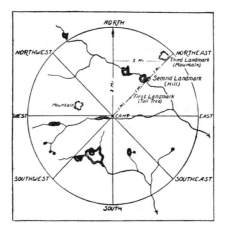

Map Showing How to Travel by Compass.

West, as well as all of the intermediate points are shown.

It is well to remember that the compass needle is effected by proximity to iron and steel, and one should not hold it close to his gun, knife or other metal object when making observations.

Ordinarily I do not wait for the needle to stop swinging, nor do I turn the compass to bring the N under the needle. I consider that midway between the limits of its motion is north, and having this point I know all of the others. For instance I am traveling northwest:

Holding the compass in my hand as nearly level as possible so that the needle swings free, I note which is North. To the right, midway between North and East is Northeast, and looking in that direction I see about a mile away a tall tree with an umbrella shaped top. I will take that for a landmark, and replacing the compass in my pocket I will walk until I reach the tree. Then I make another observation and pick another landmark farther on. It is a high, steep knoll, about a mile from the tree, and when I reach there I find a small lake lying at the foot of the hill. I cross at the outlet and climb the hill, from which point I can see the inlet, coming in from the Northwest, and a short distance up stream is another lake.

I make another observation and choose for my objective point the east side of a small mountain lying a mile farther to the Northeast. Now when I reach there I am three miles northeast of camp.

I want to see what the country is like north of my camp, and I reason that two miles west will put me almost directly north of camp. I travel that distance west, using the compass, and come out on top of an elevation, overlooking the inlet of the two lakes mentioned. I know that two miles south will take me to camp, and the stream which flows east by the camp will tell me when I have gone far enough, if I am a little to one side or the other. Also the mountain lying north of west from camp is a landmark. The map will make this clear.

Now I have learned something about the country a short distance north and east, and explorations will be conducted in the other directions. In this way I locate the nearby landmarks and will have no trouble in finding my camp if I am returning from a long trip. On long journeys I travel the same way.

Unless one desires extreme accuracy, and the woodsman seldom does, then the sun will be a good guide, and one will not need to refer to the compass so often. Even when one is using a compass there are times when he cannot see far ahead, and he can keep on traveling a straight course by watching the sun. The sun rises, in the Northern Hemisphere, somewhere south of east, and sets south of west. If you are traveling north and the time is the forenoon, you simply keep the sun shining on the back of your right shoulder; at noon, on your back, for then the sun is directly south, and in the afternoon on the back of your left shoulder.

If you must travel at night, the North Star will guide you. When you look at it you are facing north. The "Big Dipper" will show you which is the North Star, as the two stars farthest from the handle are nearly in line and are called "pointers."

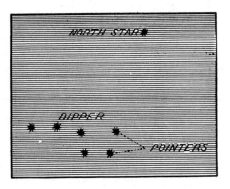

The Dipper and the North Star.

One may sometimes tell directions by the moss on the trees and other ways known to woodsmen, but they are not reliable, and I prefer to depend on the compass. The moss is supposed to grow mainly on the north side of the tree, the large limbs and rough bark on the south side, etc., but when one examines three or four trees and finds them all different, he is likely to conclude that the compass, the sun and the North Star are the most dependable.

Sometimes when one cannot see the sun or any distant objects, the wind will help out. I remember once when making a journey from one lake to another during a storm of driving snow, I could not see far enough ahead to note any object to travel towards, and it required a lot of time to look at the compass so often. Then I noted that the wind was blowing from the Northeast, and by keeping the snow skipping against the right side of my face I could travel straight west without referring to my compass. I did so and came out all right.

For me it is far more difficult to travel in a thickly settled country where I am a stranger. In such places I do not use a compass, and to a stranger all hills, bits of woodland, farmhouses, etc., look alike. Of course nobody would get lost in a country where there are so many people to direct him, but one dislikes to ask about directions. And the sportsman, hunting only a short time in a strange place is also likely to get lost, ---really lost,—for in looking for game he pays little heed to surroundings or directions. To him I can give no advice that will be of any value, except to not venture far without a guide until he learns something of the country.

It was in the mountains of Pennsylvania that I did my first hunting and trapping, for I was raised in the central part of that state. I soon learned to travel in the woods, but it was only by landmark, and I knew nothing whatever about the compass points. But after I left there and went into the bush I learned to travel by directions.

There I also learned how to lay out a trail, and found that in the wilderness I could not run a trap line without having a well marked course to follow. Especially was this necessary when tramping on snowshoes, for in the North the snow is usually in such a loose powdery condition, because of the unchanging temperature, that one does not care to break a new trail each trip, and the wind in the open country soon erases all traces of one's trail in the snow. In order to follow it again and keep on the hard tramped bottom one must have the trail well blazed.

The most common way of marking a trail is by chipping spots on the sides of trees. In the thick bush it is often the only way, as brush are scarce in many places and the smaller undergrowth gets snowed under. Ordinarily it is a good way, but in the evergreen bush, the snow laden limbs sometimes droop enough to hide the marks, and a driving snow storm will sometimes

hide the marks effectually, by sticking the snow
on the trunks of the trees. For these reasons I
prefer, when possible, to mark on the larger
brush by cutting them half off and bending them
aside, the tops pointing away from the trail.
This makes a mark that may be seen readily no
matter which way one is traveling. I am aware
though that it would not answer in the higher

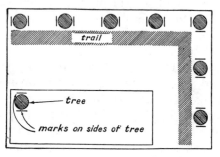

Diagram Showing How to Mark a Trail.

portions of the western mountains, where the
snow falls very deep, but for the Canadian bush
and the wilder parts of the Northern States, it is
O. K.

A trail should always be so marked that it
may be followed each way. In other words, one
should mark on two sides of the tree. It should
be run as straight as possible, but where it is
necessary to turn, the bend should be indicated

by the marks, that is to say, the blazes on the trees should point out the course. The diagram will make this clear.

The Northern Indians seldom mark their trails, in fact, they seldom have any. They can always find their traps because they know the country and seldom go off into the thick bush away from streams and other landmarks, unless there is snow on the ground. In that case they can follow the snowshoe trail in the thick bush, for there, where there is never much wind, the trail will be discernible a long time after it is broken out. It can be obliterated only by a very heavy fall of snow, but out in the open country a trail may be entirely lost in a single day, by drifting snow. The Indian's trail is always crooked. He follows the hollows and cares not if they lead him out of his course; another will bring him back, and it is usually no farther around one side of a hill than over it, while the walk may be made with less effort.

Those who are much in the woods have invariably adopted the long swinging gait of the bushman. It is an easy method of walking, less tiring than the straight, stiff stride of the one who walks on smooth ground or city pavements. This gait comes naturally to any one doing much walking in the bush, and especially to those who use snowshoes. The woodsman keeps up a steady easy walk from morning until night, as a rule not very fast, but he covers a lot of territory in a day. If going far, one should not walk too fast, nor should he take a longer step than ordinary. It is endurance that counts most when traveling in the bush, and endurance and speed are seldom found in combination.

CHAPTER XVI.

TRAVELING LIGHT.

HIS advice is not intended for the tenderfoot, for he should never attempt to "rough it," and that is just what it means to "travel light," for when making long journeys overland, carrying the camping outfit and food on one's back, one must leave behind all of those little articles which are so necessary for the comfort of the tender one. The instructions given here are for the hardy outdoor man, inexperienced in bush life, but with a desire to learn of the methods employed. I give my own methods of traveling and camping out, and if others think they have better ways, they should remember that we woodsmen are all cranks and that their modes might seem as absurd to me as mine do to them.

For such trips into the woods one must of a necessity lighten his outfit as much as possible, and every article that is not absolutely necessary should be dispensed with. And it is astonishing what a very little bit of duffle is really needed for camping out. On my initial trip of this kind, if I remember rightly, I carried a double barrel gun weighing $7\frac{1}{2}$ pounds, a few shells for same, a 4 pound double bit axe, a blanket for bedding (it was early fall) and another light one for a shelter, a frying pan, about 11 inches in diameter, a tea pail, a small stew kettle, a knife, fork and table spoon, and all of the food necessary for a five days' trip, minus the baking powder for making the bread, this having been forgotten. This outfit, with the exception of the axe and gun, was done up in one of the blankets and carried with a tump line. I soon found it a poor arrangement for tramping through a rough and unknown country, and my progress was slow.

However I managed to get along fairly well but soon learned that I was packing too much of an outfit, and the articles which were really necessary were far heavier than they should be. With an axe in one hand, a gun in the other, and a comparatively heavy pack hanging from my head, you readers can imagine that I had some trouble in the thick brush and dense swamps, and much of the ground was of that nature. I also missed the baking powder very much and tried sour dough bread, but having no soda and only sugar and salt, it certainly did not rise very well. I also lost a lot of time in fixing up my pack and in tying up each kind of food in a separate package, all of which I learned to do in a different way afterwards, but this knowledge was not all gained on one trip.

Now for an ordinary camping trip I carry an outfit something like this: A sheet of heavy drill (not duck) measuring about 5 x 7 feet with triangular ends and with loops sewn on the edges about 16 inches apart. This was the most satisfactory shelter out of several styles which I made and tried out. I carry a light, single bit axe now, in preference to the heavy one, and find that if it has a good length handle and is kept sharp it will do practically as good work. I take a small frying pan, No. 0 size, which has a square socket for using a wood handle. It is very light and takes up very little space. I also take a small tinned pail or a quart can fitted with a haywire bail. If I wish to have a boiled meal occasionally I take a small tin kettle also, but when I wish to go very light, I leave this article behind. Knife, fork and spoon are also dispensed with. A flattened stick answers for a spoon, a pointed one makes a good fork, and the sheath knife answers for cutting everything from slicing bacon to whittling shavings to kindle a fire with. I use a single blanket, a large woolen one in spring, summer and fall, and a woven rabbit skin robe in winter. I also carry a pair of sheepskin moccasins in winter to wear when I get up to fix the fire.

My food is all put up in little cloth bags, of which I always keep an abundant supply. The flour is measured out before I leave camp and to each quart I add two teaspoonfuls of baking powder, Price's preferred, and one teaspoonful of salt. This is well mixed with the flour and everything else prepared for the start on the evening before.

The food which I carry on such trips usually consists of only flour, bacon (or salt pork), tea, coffee and butter, some dried fruits, some sugar and a little salt, and if the trip is to be of several days' duration, a mess or two of beans or split peas. I measure out a sufficient portion for each day's use and then add one or two days' supplies for emergencies. Matches are carried in a Marble's waterproof case. I also carry a small file and sharpening stone for the axe and some pieces of strong cord. In winter I always carry a few rabbit snares and in summer a fish line and hooks, but I never depend on fish or game when camping out.

I carry this outfit in a duck pack sack, using the shoulder straps, and sometimes where the ground is smooth I use the head strap to relieve my shoulders. For this use I think the pack sack is superior to any other packing arrangement, anyway it is the best of those which I have used. In making up the pack I first fold the blanket into a flat form about two feet square, or just the proper size to lay nicely in the sack. This goes next to my back and makes a nice pad for the pack. The cooking outfit is put up in a cloth sack and slipped in the bottom of the pack behind the blanket. The food goes on top of this and then the drill shelter. The axe I carry in a leather case usually tucked in the pack, head down, but sometimes attached to the top and sometimes slung by a strap from my shoulder. It is least in the way when in the pack.

A rabbit skin blanket, if simply folded or stuffed in loose, will fill the ordinary pack sack, so I fold it up and roll it tight inside of the shelter cloth, tying it with cord. Even then it makes a rather bulky package.

Traveling in the bush in fall and late spring is pleasant, especially in spring. At that time the ground is mostly bare and is cleaner than at any other time. There is none of the rank vegetation which covers the ground so thickly in summer, and the dead grass and weeds of the fall previous have been pressed down flat by the winter's snow so that they do not interfere with walking. The nights are also pleasant at this time of the year, and it does not require a large fire to keep you comfortable. It is just as nice in the fall, but because of the dying vegetation the walking is not as good.

It will probably interest some to know how I use the outfit described. When camping out I always select a camping site some time towards night, usually about an hour before dark if possible. During the winter one need only look for wood and shelter, but in the fall, spring and summer one must also look for water. I seldom go far away from a stream or lake if I find one late in the afternoon, unless I know that I will find water elsewhere before night. I select a sheltered place for the camp, among small evergreens if possible, and keep as far away from high hills as possible, for in such places the wind is uncertain.

Having found a nice dry smooth spot, I pitch my shelter at an angle of about 45 degrees, facing leeward. A straight pole is cut and slipped through the loops at the upper edge of the shelter cloth and the ends fastened to trees. The bottom is fastened by driving stakes through the loops, and the triangular corners are stretched out to form ends on the shelter and are fastened in the same way.

I carpet the inside of the shelter with evergreen boughs and lay a small log in front. The fire is made about six feet from the front of the

15

shelter, and if possible, with a large log, stump, rock or bank of earth behind it. This will act as a reflector and throw the heat into the camp, and if a log it will also hold fire in case I sleep too soundly.

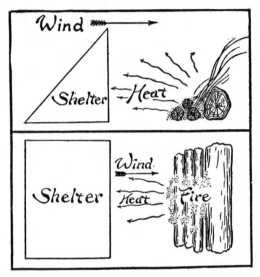

The Relative Positions of Shelter and Campfire.

If it is nearly dark I cut and carry the wood for the night before pitching the shelter, as I do not like to use the axe much after dark, but I have cut the night's supply of wood by moonlight on more than one occasion. If there is plenty of time I leave this wood gathering for the last.

It is far more pleasant for two to camp together, and there is less danger. If there are two, one can cut and gather the wood while the other makes a comfortable camp and starts the evening meal.

Usually the menu consists of baking powder bread, butter sometimes, bacon, and black tea. I fry the bacon first by raking a few coals out before the fire and placing the frying pan over them, supported by two chunks of green wood. While the bacon is frying I mix the bread. This I do in the top of the flour bag. Opening it up as wide as possible I gouge a hole down into the center of the flour and pour in the proper amount of water, the flour having been prepared before starting out, and then with a flattened stick I stir the flour into the water until I have a ball of dough, which I turn into the hot bacon grease in the frying pan, the bacon having been removed. I then flatten it out as much as possible and put fresh coals under the pan. The dough absorbs the grease, and when it has baked to a nice brown on the under side I turn it over and bake the other side. While the bread is baking I also prepare the tea, and in a half hour or less after I have commenced the cooking I have a meal. The beans, peas and fruit are cooked after night and eaten in the morning. The game which is taken along the trail is also cooked at night.

In winter when the snow is deep one must camp on top of the snow. I tramp the snow down solid with my snowshoes before making the camp, and also make a bed of small green logs to build the fire on. Balsam is best for the purpose, but I prefer to use some other wood because of the danger of breaking an axe in frozen balsam wood. I will remark right here that in cold weather I always make a little fire, if only of birch bark and draw the frost from the blade of the axe before cutting the night's wood, for it is far more likely to break if it is cold. A broken axe, when one is far from the reach of help, is a serious matter, if it is cold weather.

I pile the wood by the side of the shelter, where it is easily reached. It will require nearly a half cord of dry wood for a cold night, for the fire will need replenishing about every one and a half hours. In the North, the best woods are dead poplar, tamarack, birch, spruce and jack pine, with a few chunks of green birch among the dead wood. I also keep some fine dry wood handy to use in case the fire becomes very low before I awake. Standing wood is always drier than that which lays on the ground. For the cooking fire use hardwood, as it burns to coals while soft woods burn to ashes.

It is difficult for the amateur to get a full night's sleep when camping out, or anyway it was that way with me. After fixing the fire I would not feel sleepy, and by the time I would fall into a doze the fire would need attention again. One soon gets used to this, however, and can get up and fix the fire and be asleep again in five minutes. In the morning he will not know how often he was up. It is also difficult to sleep with a cap on one's head, but that is necessary. A wool toque is best during cold weather, but one can become so used to it that he can even keep a hat on his head all night.

In the morning before leaving the camping spot, I stand on end all of the wood which has been left over, and many times I have camped again in the same place and was glad to have a little wood all ready cut. This is often the case when on a regular route of travel, such as the trap line.

If you are camping out while trapping, always set your extra trap (most trappers carry one with them) in the most likely looking place near the camp, and you can take it along with you the next day if you do not wish to leave it setting. I remember once, while trapping with a partner, we made camp in a thicket of evergreens near the lake shore. It was quite late in the evening, and when pard suggested that we set a trap along the shore, I objected because I knew that it would take all of the time to get the wood before dark. As it was, we had to carry the wood to camp in the dark, but in the morning I was sorry that we had not set the trap there just the same, for a large lynx had walked the ice along the shore not more than a rod from where pard wanted to set the trap. "You see there," said pard, "if you had let me set that trap we would have had a lynx this morning," and I had to admit that I had made a mistake.

In winter one does not look for water when selecting a camping place, for one can get any amount of it by melting snow. The only things to look for are shelter, wood and evergreen boughs for a bed.

The foregoing is my regular way of traveling and camping out, but one may, if he wishes to put up with some discomfort, travel even lighter. I have at times omitted the shelter, and I have known the Indians to camp out without blankets or shelter when the temperature was far below zero, but none for mine. I also sometimes leave the frying pan behind, and in such cases I make bread by winding the dough around sticks and standing them up by the side of the fire. The bacon is toasted or broiled by fixing it on pointed sticks. I do not like to do this, however, as all of the grease is lost.

In summer I have left both blanket and axe behind. I kept a fire over night by burning what dead wood I could pick up, or drag to the camp, and as the weather was reasonably warm I slept comfortably without the blanket. I will say, though, that some of my most unpleasant camping trips were summer ones.

CHAPTER XVII.

TANNING FURS AND BUCKSKIN.

ANNING is an art, but almost any person who takes an interest in it, and has a desire to learn can do fair work after a few trials, and after a while, if he experiments in an intelligent way, and learns the principles of tanning and the action of the various chemicals, he will be able to do as good work as that done by custom tanners, but should not bank too much on making a success right at the start. Experimenting in this line is interesting and there are always some cheap skins and furs that one may try out his methods on. For instance, there is the woodchuck, or groundhog. His skin when properly tanned makes a strong, durable leather and in many places they are shot and never skinned, or if the hunter does remove the pelt he stretches it up on the side of the barn or outbuilding and leaves it there to rot. It has no market value and I would advise those who wish to learn tanning to experiment on woodchuck hides.

At present almost all furs are high, and I would not advise anybody to make their first attempt at tanning furs on a skin that has any great market value, but one can get small opossums, damaged muskrats and other furs of like value. The common house cat is a good one to experiment with, and I have seen some very nice fur work made from the skins of the common tabby. One man, to whom I am indebted for the most of what I know about tanning, buys up house cats for a few cents each and makes the skins up into sleigh robes. Black cats make a very nice lap-robe and even the colored ones make nice robes if the colors are well matched.

I propose to give here some simple modes of tanning furs and buckskin, and the methods given are the best that I know of. I will speak of buckskin first.

Tanning is a loosening up of the fiber of the skin, making it soft and pliable, and so treating it that it will remain in that condition. At the same time it must not be overdone, for if a pelt is overtanned it will not wear well. One should be especially careful when using such powerful chemicals as sulphuric acid, as it is very easy to burn a skin when using this medium.

Before a deerskin can be tanned for leather it must be fleshed and grained. Make a graining beam as follows: Get a hardwood log, eight feet long and eight inches in diameter. It must be free of knots at one end. Bore two one and a half inch holes near one end and fit in a pair of legs. Now smooth off the top for a distance of three feet, leaving it slightly rounding. It is best to use a plane after the rough has been hewn off with an axe, as the log must be perfectly smooth to prevent cutting the skin.

A graining knife must be provided next. I have grained hides with a flat bar of metal with square edges, having the ends wound with cloth so it would not hurt my hands, but a far better article can be made from an old half-round file, and if you propose doing much work of this kind I would advise making one. I used a file about twenty inches long and ground all of the rough off. Then I drove a short hand-fitting handle onto the tang and heated the other end and hammered a short tang on it. I then fitted on a short oval handle crosswise, as shown in the cut, and riveted the end of the file over a washer. The edges of the file were ground square and sharp. This made an ideal tool for graining.

A green skin is easily grained. Lay it on the smooth end of the beam, hair side up and hair pointing away from the elevated end. Seat yourself on a stool or chair at the elevated end of the beam, draw the neck of the skin over the end and hold it firmly in place by pressing your

The Graining Knife, the Graining Beam and Mode of Using.

chest against it. Now grasping the graining knife firmly, press it down hard on the hair of the hide and push away from you, towards the low end of the beam. The hair and a strip of the thin outside skin in which the hair grows will slip off. That is the way it is done, and one must go over the entire skin in that way; not a particle of the grain or scarf skin should be left on the hide.

I forgot to say that the skin must be carefully fleshed before it is grained. The easiest way is to stretch it up on a wall and peel the flesh off with a knife.

A dry skin must be thoroughly soaked before it can be fleshed and grained. Let it lay in warm water twenty-four hours, then add a handful or two of slacked lime and let it remain another twenty-four hours. After graining wash the skin in clear water and put it in warm soapsuds, working it thoroughly with the hands for a half-hour. This is to remove the lime. The skin is then ready for tanning.

There are many ways of tanning buckskin, but here is one that I have found very good. Take a tablespoonful each of white vitriol, alum and salt and dissolve it in just sufficient water to cover the hide. Soak the skin in this twenty-four hours, a longer time if the skin is a very heavy one. Then remove it, wring it as dry as possible and if no dense spots are seen, hang it in the sun and apply to the flesh side, with a brush, a half pint of curriers' oil. It may be procured from tanners. Butter is also very good and is easier washed out afterwards, but more expensive. Let it hang about two days, then stretch it out on a floor and with a scouring brush and warm soapsuds scour out all of the oil that is possible to get out. Now wring out all of the water and dry it in the sun. Here is where the work comes in. It must be pulled and rubbed vigorously all of the time while it is drying or it will dry hard. If you use plenty of elbow grease it will come out as soft and pliable as a piece of chamois skin, and will always remain so.

My only objection to this method is that the leather so made is always of an oily nature and gets soiled very easily. But one may wash it at any time in warm soapy water and the leather will be soft again when dry.

In case one does not wish to use oil, the following mode is all O. K.: When the skin is taken from the tanning liquor, wring it out and pull it until it is dry, then stretch it up over a smudge of rotten hardwood and smoke it a whole day. This answers the same purpose as the oil, namely, it keeps the skin from drying hard after wetting. It is best to smoke it in some outbuilding, and in the woods one can make a small wigwam out of bark, to retain the smoke. Do not let the fire burn so that it makes a heat.

Here is a very simple method and it is my opinion that it is just as good as any: Having fleshed and grained the skin as before, provide a wooden trough and folding the skin lengthwise place it in same. Now take a pail of hot water and shave a bar of ordinary laundry soap and stir it until dissolved. Then pour it over the skin in the trough and let it soak until tanned. Try squeezing water through it occasionally, for when the water will pass through it is tanned. Then wring it out and pull it dry as in the other method. Now if the thick portion along the back does not get as soft as desired put it back in the trough, leaving only the hard portion in the liquor. After it is pulled and worked again until dry and soft smoke it thoroughly. I have seen deer skin tanned this way that was as soft as leather could possibly be made, but such leather is not good for moccasins or mittens, as it will not wear well, and when one wishes it to stand considerable wear he should be careful not to overtan it.

The Indians sometimes use this soap method, but the real Indian tan is quite different. It is done with the brains of the animal itself. Dry the brains gently by the side of the fire then tie them in a cloth and boil them one hour. Squeeze as much as possible through the cloth and when it is just cool enough to allow one to put his hands in it, immerse the grained skin and work it thoroughly with the hands until the liquor cools. Then heat it up again and repeat the soaking. When tanned, remove and wring as dry as possible and then wash it in strong soapsuds, and wringing it out again, hang it up to dry. While still damp grease it lightly with butter or some animal oil. Keep pulling and stretching it, first one way and then the other, until it is perfectly dry, rubbing it well between the hands if it shows a tendency to get hard anywhere. If left in this condition it would dry hard again after wetting, and must be thoroughly smoked to prevent this. The smoke will also give it a yellow color. The Indian tan is one of the best as the leather gets nice and soft and wears well.

Tanning furs as a rule is not so difficult. I mean that there is not so much work connected with it. Here is one of the best methods that I know of: Flesh the skin carefully, then soak it from two to six hours (according to the weight of the skin) in the following liquor: Four gallons of cold, soft water, one-half ounce borax, one-half pint salt and one ounce of sulphuric acid. This will prepare it for the tanning liquor and set the hair securely. Now take two gallons of cold, soft water, one-fourth pound of pulverized oxalic acid and one quart of salt. Put the skins in this and leave them there until there are no more dense spots to be seen. It will take about forty-eight hours for a catskin or other fur of the same thickness, and a longer time for heavier furs. When tanned remove them and wring dry, then hang them in the shade and pull them while drying so that they do not get hard. This tan is proof against moths and is a very nice one. The method is good for tanning skins for rugs.

Here is a method of tanning woodchuck skins for leather, taken from The Farmers' Tanning Guide, which we sell for 25 cents:

"Put the skins into a bucket of ashes and water, let them remain until the hair comes out easily, then take the hair off; put the skins into soft soap until the lye eats the flesh off; then take them out and rub dry over a smoke."

While still living at home I knew of farmer boys using this method to make leather for ball covers, and it made very nice soft leather. I do not see any reason why it could not be used for many other purposes.

I will give one more method of tanning small furs, as follows:

Flesh the skin and clean the fur by washing

with warm water and soap, rinsing with clear water. Take a quarter of a pound of salt, the same of powdered alum and half an ounce of borax. Dissolve this in hot water and add sufficient rye meal to make a thick paste and spread it thickly on the flesh side. Then fold the skin lengthwise, flesh side in, and let it remain in an airy, shady place from one to two weeks, depending on the thickness of the skin. Then remove the paste and wash and dry the skin. If it is a heavy skin it may require a second application of the paste. After drying, pull it over a beam and work it between the hands until it is as soft as desired.

To give furs a nice, fluffy, lifelike look after tanning and to liven up old manufactured furs, take Paris white and brush it through the fur, using a stiff brush. Hot poplar sawdust is also good for this purpose.

Now these methods of tanning are all good and by following directions carefully one can do nice work, but I have never known anybody to do really good tanning at the first trial, so as before advised, do not experiment on a valuable skin. The trouble with most people is that they do not realize how much working is really needed while the skin is drying and are likely to neglect this very important matter. I would ad-

16

vise also that after a skin is tanned, if there is a spot that will not get soft, moisten that part again with the tan liquor and put it through the same process as before. This applies to all of the methods given. I will say also that the various tans for deerskins are also good for moose and caribou, but these heavier skins require a longer time in each process.

I spoke before of using catskins for robes. Many persons wonder where and how they can procure one of the Indian rabbit blankets. It is my opinion that one could make a fine sleeping bag to take the place of one of these rabbit skin blankets, by lining an ordinary woolen blanket with tanned house cat skins and then sewing it up into the form of a bag, fur side in.

Many other useful articles can be made by the hunter, if he once masters tanning. He can make his own moccasins and camp slippers, mittens and all similar articles. As everybody knows, in a cold climate fur goods are also useful and valuable, and it is well to know how to do the work even though you may never want to practice it.

CHAPTER XVIII.

PRESERVING GAME, FISH AND HIDES.

 REALIZE that I could write a very lengthy chapter under this heading without overdoing it, but it is not my intention to go into detail regarding the handling of raw furs. What I do wish to write about is the handling of big game and its preservation by hunting parties, the preserving of game heads, skinning for mounting, drying meat and the curing of deer skins.

As a boy, I was much interested in big game hunting and my one great ambition was to become a successful hunter and trapper. I read all the available hunting literature and noted that the drawings of the oldtime hunters invariably showed a large sheath knife dangling from the belt. I supposed that the knife was absolutely necessary to use in cutting the throat of big game after killing. I don't know how I got the idea, but I was surprised afterward to learn that few big game hunters practiced that.

What I did learn about handling game was that one should lose no time in dressing it after killing, and that it should be kept out of the way of the blue bottle flies if the weather is warm. Anyway one should remove the entrails immediately or gas will accumulate and the flavor of the meat will be ruined. The congested blood should also be removed as quickly as possible.

Game killed with the old time, black powder gun, of large caliber usually bled freely, but the modern high power rifle with soft nose bullets gives such a tremendous shock that the blood thickens in a mass. As a rule, one will find a large mass of this congested blood about the lung cavity, if the game has been hit anywhere about the shoulders as it usually is. This blood should be removed and the cavity wiped clean with a dry cloth, if possible, as soon as the internal organs are out of the way.

In removing the entrails, split the skin and flesh on the belly, not too far, and loosen the intestines at the vent, also cut the gullet as far up above the stomach as possible, then remove the entrails. If the game is to be cut up on the spot the skin may be opened on the belly all the way to the vent and the pelvic bone split with the hunting axe or the point of a heavy knife. If it is to be transported some distance only a small opening should be made and it should be tied shut again after the entrails are removed. This is easily done by punching a few small holes through the edge of the skin with the point of a knife and tying with string.

I believe that deer hunters generally hang deer up by the hind legs in order to dress them. It is all right to do so, but I could dress a deer while one is getting a pole to hang it with and any way the deer should not be allowed to hang long head down.

The proper way to hang deer is as shown in the photo. I give several reasons for this, the most important being that when hung head down the blood drains into the lung cavity and remains there and spoils some of the meat. When hung as shown in the photo it will drain out of the cavity, and there is no place to collect rain and snow. Another thing is that the hair pointing backwards acts as a raincoat when the animal is hung head up.

Hunting is usually done after the weather has become quite cool and there is very little danger of the game being fly-blown at that time, but if a warm day comes, it is wise to make a few small smudges where the smoke will protect the meat from the blue-bottles.

Such game as deer, black bear and other animals are commonly suspended from a horizontal pole by the side of the camp, but with larger game such methods are not practicable. Occasions are very rare when one would have an

The Correct Way to Hang Deer.

opportunity of bringing a moose or elk out of the forest, intact, and few hunters think of doing so. Such game is dressed and skinned on the spot where killed and the best meat is trimmed from the bones and packed into camp. Among northern hunters if the game is not killed too far from home or camp it is a common practice to quarter it and put the meat on a scaffold, covered with the skin. There are few large carnivorous animals in the North and if there are no wolverines it is not likely to be disturbed. It must be well covered though to protect it from the moose birds. There where the weather is so cold, the flesh will keep all winter long, frozen as hard as a pine knot, and the hunter can pack it into camp at his convenience.

As a rule it is the head of the game that the sportsman values most highly, especially when the said game is a large bull moose, elk, caribou or deer and in case it is a bear, the head and hide. If he is after the head some instructions regarding the care of same may not come amiss.

Many taxidermists prefer to skin the heads themselves and if the weather is cold and a good taxidermist within easy reach it is best to not skin it at all.

Before going farther, I will say that if the head must be skinned, a few photographs of

same viewed from different sides will aid the
taxidermist greatly. So also will some measurements, and one should measure the muzzle in
several places, also the circumference of the
head just in front of the ears, and of the neck
close behind the head and near the shoulders.

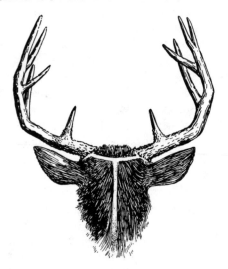

Showing How to Skin a Deer Head for Mounting.

If the weather is the least bit warm, if one
must transport the head far, or if it will be a
considerable length of time before the head can
be placed in the taxidermist's care, it should be
skinned, otherwise it may heat and the hair slip

off in spots. The following is the proper method of skinning a head for mounting.

Rip the skin about the neck close up to the shoulders; then split it on the back of the neck to a point between the antlers, from there to the base of each antler, as shown in the cut. Now skin the neck carefully, keeping the skin clean. When you reach the head cut the ears off close to the skull. Be very careful in skinning about the eyes as the eyelids must not be injured. The same applies to the mouth and nostrils as the skin of the lips is necessary and the nostrils could not be finished up nicely without enough of the lining to turn in so that no cuts will show. The ears should then be skinned out to the tips.

After skinning the head leave the skin with the flesh side out and hang it in a shady place to dry. Sprinkle it well with fine salt or if you have it, alum and salt. Treated thus there is not the least danger that the skin will spoil.

All flesh should be carefully cleaned from the skull by scraping. Make an opening into the base of it and remove the brains. Some sportsmen saw the skull through lengthwise leaving one horn on each half and this is a great aid in packing, but a saw is not often to be found in a hunting camp.

Large and fine specimens of game fish are frequently mounted on panels. It is difficult to preserve fish and about the only way is to skin them and place in brine until they can be turned over to the taxidermist. Before skinning a fish note the colors and remember them if possible, for fish change color rapidly after death. Also measure accurately its length, width and thickness.

Mounted on a panel only one side of the fish is shown, so if one side is more perfect than the other, turn this side down and on the imperfect side cut the skin just behind the gills down the belly to the tail and up to the back. Loosen this flap and turn it back out of the way. Then skin the body carefully, cutting it loose at the fins, tail and head. Leave the head in the skin but remove the brains through an opening at the base; also remove the eyes, having noted their color. The skin may now be placed in strong brine.

Fish grow soft rapidly and the sportsman who wishes to preserve his fish for food even a day or two must use care or they will not come through in good condition. They should not be allowed to remain in either the sunshine or the water. Dress them as quiclky as possible and wipe clean of blood and slime, then pack them in the basket, back down, between layers of cold, damp moss, from some cold spring water. In this way they will come through nicely.

Fishermen, hunters, trappers and others sometimes wish to put up fresh water fish for winter use and this is easily done. Dress the fish by splitting them on the back, then wash clean and roll in salt. Place them in a wooden vessel in a cool place for several days, then turn them out on the floor and let the brine drain off. Clean the vessel and put the fish back. Cover them again with brine made strong enough to carry an egg or a potato. Trout preserved in this way are excellent. There are also methods of dry curing fish, used much by the Indians, but I do not know how it is done.

Where big game is not plentiful, woodsmen who spend the entire winter season in the wilds sometimes have the luck to kill big game in the early fall and knowing that they will have little chance for finding game after cold weather sets in. may wish to preserve the meat. Again one may be able to kill game in the spring and wish to preserve it during warm weather. It is then that the knowledge of "jerking" meat is useful.

The common method practiced by the older hunters was to trim all of the flesh from the bones, cutting it into strips about an inch in thickness. This was placed inside of the skin and from a pint to a quart of salt, depending on the size of the animal, was well worked into the meat. The skin was then folded over the meat and left in that condition about twenty-four hours.

In the meantime a square scaffold of poles was erected, the poles being placed about a foot apart and four or five feet above the ground. Small straight sticks were then placed crosswise and the meat was spread out on the scaffold. A smudge of hardwood was then made under the scaffold and the meat was smoked thoroughly for several days, until it was shrunken up to a very small bulk, and was very hard. If this meat was kept in a dry place, well up from the ground it would keep indefinitely. Pemmican is meat so treated, pounded into shreds, and mixed with tallow and a few dried berries or other fruit.

Instead of salting the meat before drying some hunters prefer to boil it sharply for a half hour in strong salt water before placing it on the scaffold. Others simply dip the meat into the boiling water and I believe the Indians do not use salt at all. I presume that all these ways are good, anyway I know a man who once hunted for the market and often dried venison by first boiling it and then smoking. This meat was sold in the cities for a good price.

It is not necessary to do all of the smoking at one time, but if there are blue bottle flies about, the meat must be placed out of their reach when there is no smoke going. The fire should be slow and the smoke thin, so it will penetrate the meat. Do not try to hurry it. If there is any wind, stand bark up against the scaffold to prevent the smoke being blown away.

I will say something about the care of hides before closing this article. Many hunters like to have deer and bear skins tanned for rugs and mats or to hang on the wall. Some sportsmen also like deer skins tanned with the hair off (buckskin) for table covers, and I will say that they are very nice for that purpose. As big game animals are becoming more and more rare each year in many parts of the country it is up to every big game hunter to get all possible out of his hunting and nothing should be wasted. But many fine skins are lost each season by the owner's lack of knowledge regarding the care of same.

A skin to be preserved in good condition for tanning should be removed from the animal as soon as possible after killing. If the game is of the deer family, cut the skin loose around the knee joints and the neck (if the head is not t/ be mounted) and rip it down the belly to th tail. Rip the skin down the back of the hina legs to the base of the tail and down the inside of the front legs to the body, then forward to the point of the brisket. Then remove the skin carefully with a sharp knife, keeping it perfectl clear of flesh and fat, and as clean otherwise as possible. It should be stretched up in a cool, shady place and allowed to dry slowly. It must not be allowed to become wet at any time. Do not salt it unless absolutely necessary.

Bears and other animals which are to be made up into rugs with mounted heads are skinned in the same way except that the skin is not cut around the neck, being split out to the point of the lower jaw and the head skinned along with the body. The feet and legs are also skinned out entire, the split being run out to the center on the bottom of each foot.

One thing more—do not throw away the feet of the deer, elk, moose, caribou, sheep, etc. They make beautiful ink wells, match holders, ash trays, gun racks, and feet for stands, foot stools, etc. Any taxidermist can make them up into such articles.

CHAPTER XIX.

MISCELLANEOUS SUGGESTIONS.

N glancing over the previous chapters I find that there are a number of woodcraft wrinkles which I meant to speak of, but which were forgotten at the time. I want to mention also many little thing which are worth knowing, but which alone were not sufficient for a chapter. I will talk first of the common ailments which are most likely to afflict the lone camper, and give simple treatments for them.

SICKNESS IN CAMP. The most common ills which are likely to overtake the camper, barring cuts, bruises, broken bones and other accidental hurts, are colds, diarrhoea, cramps, sore throat, toothache, sprains, sore feet and snow blindness. One should bear in mind the possibility of such afflictions and should include in his outfit a few simple remedies. Here are a few which should be taken:

Epsom salts, quinine (in capsules, or, what I like better, laxative bromo quinine), carbolic acid, turpentine, essence of peppermint, ginger, mustard, vinegar, peroxide, carbolated vaseline and arnica. Some of these may not come under the heading of drugs, but they are used as such just the same.

"An ounce of preventoin is worth a pound of cure." One cannot take as good care of himself when in the woods as he can when in town, but such care is not needed. If one will keep the bowels open, avoid those acts which usually bring on colds, such as overheating and then sitting down in a cool, shady place, and not sit or lie on the damp ground, then there will be little sickness, but one cannot always follow these rules.

One of the most common afflictions is constipation. It may be relieved by means of epsom salts and a change of diet, eating especially plenty of stewed fruit. Prunes are excellent in such cases. Drink plenty of pure water.

Colds are another common ill. As a rule, each person has his pet way of treating a cold. I use quinine, although many people say it is not good to use much of it. Laxative bromo quinine is very good; follow the directions on the box. If you have the pure quinine tablets or capsules, take in connection a dose of the salts. Before going to bed drink plenty of hot ginger infusion and cover up well so you will sweat. Do this only when you are certain that you will keep well covered during the night, for if you sweat and then throw the blankets off you are certain to catch more cold. In case a cold settles in the chest, draw the inflammation to the surface with mustard or a turpentine or kerosene saturated flannel. After using this, place over the sore part a soft cloth lightly spread with carbolated vaseline.

For internal cramps, mix ginger in very hot water and drink it; also take a few drops of essence of peppermint in water.

For diarrhœa, drink a mixture of flour, water and cinnamon, also take light doses of some common astringent at intervals of several hours, until relieved. An infusion of oak bark makes a powerful astringent; blackberry root is also good.

For burns or scalds, apply moistened soda and bind with a cloth. I know of nothing which equals this, but flour is also good.

For sore throat, tie a piece of fat bacon on the throat and leave it over night. Wear the bandage awhile after the pork is removed. Gargle the throat frequently with one part peroxide and two parts water. Tincture of iron, diluted, is also good.

To relieve toothache, hold in the mouth a solution of hot vinegar and salt. The best remedy I have ever found, however, is cold water

7

held in the mouth. It is severe at first, but soon quiets and numbs the nerve.

Cuts, bites of animals and other open wounds should be washed out with warm water to which a few drops of carbolic acid has been added, about four drops to a quart of water. After washing, apply a bandage and carbolated vaseline. If the wound is a large one, bring the edges together and hold them that way with strips of adhesive plaster. Do not close the wound entirely. Leave one end open for the escape of pus, especially if a deep cut.

Sore feet are sometimes caused by wearing moccasins when one is used to stiff shoes. This is not serious, as one's feet soon get used to the change, but it may be relieved by bathing them in hot water, then in cold water to which some soda has been added.

Trappers, explorers, prospectors and others, who go long distances into the wilderness and spend many months there, are very likely to become afflicted with scurvy. This disease is caused by eating too much prepared food, especially salt pork, but it may be relieved easily by eating fresh raw vegetables, fresh meats and fish, and by not eating salt or grease in the food. Vinegar is one of the best remedies for scurvy, lime juice is also good. I knew two trappers, brothers, who went a long distance into the northern bush and spent the entire season there. They subsisted largely on salt pork and as a result both got the scurvy. One of them cured himself by eating boiled fresh fish, without salt, but the other had never eaten fish and could not do so. His brother therefore gathered him a supply of firewood and then set out for the settlements to get medicine. It was early spring and the snow melted through the day, freezing hard at night. The man was in a hurry for his brother's life depended on his exertions, so he traveled each day as long as he could see to go lying down at night with his wet moccasins on and without a fire. The result was that while he returned in time to save his brother he took cold on his lungs and was sick all summer. The doctor told him that a single bottle of vinegar would have cured both of them of the scurvy and saved all of the privation and consequent sickness.

In northern countries one is likely to become snowblind in the early spring when the snow is melting. Wearing a pair of colored glasses will cure it, but one does not always have the glasses. In such cases rub charcoal or soot about the eyes and on the nose. A pair of spectacles of bark or leather having only small slits or apertures for the wearer to see through are also good.

FIXING UP A PERMANENT CAMP. Usually, after one has lived in a log camp for some time, he sees where he can improve it in many ways, and it gives one something to do on rainy days, work which I never regret having done, for I like comfort when it is to be had. As a rule, the trapper is content for awhile to sit on the edge of the bunk or on the floor eating his meals out of the frying pan, but it is not necessary to do so, for a table is easily made. I build a stationary one along one side of the camp by driving two stout stakes, placing crosspieces to the logs of the wall and fastening split and hewn boards on them.

A box or cupboard must also be made for the food supplies, as they are sure to be ruined by mice if these little mischief makers can gain access. I use a covered box and make it tight, for the little black wood mice can get through a very small crack. However, it is the larger species which do the most mischief, as the small kind eat nothing but meat. It is no use to try to keep food from them by hanging it up, for I have seen them climbing down a two-foot codfish line to get into my flour.

One can make this box from split and hewn boards or if it is summer he can make a frame of wood and cover it with sheets of bark.

If one is going to spend a whole season in a log camp, as when on a trapping trip, it is a good idea to have a few tools for wood-working, especially if he is going in some time before the trapping season. A small block plane is a very useful tool; a small panel saw is handy, and one can find use for a drawing knife and an auger.

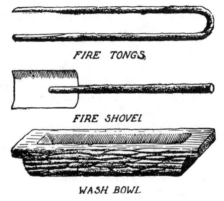

FIRE TONGS,

FIRE SHOVEL

WASH BOWL

Easily Made and Useful Articles.

Of course, such things are not necessary, but they are useful. On rainy or stormy days one can make stretching boards, shelves for his camp, a box for furs, snowshoe frames, toboggan, snow shovel, axe handles, etc. I also make a wooden bowl for a washbasin by hollowing out a block of wood. Many other things will suggest themselves. If one goes into camp in the summer, he can make many useful things out of birch bark, such as receptacles for food, washtub, etc.

I once fixed up a camp very nicely by lining it entirely with birch bark. I made a cupboard of split, hewn and planed cedar boards, and even put a ceiling in the cabin.

How many of the readers know how to make a bake oven? They are easily made, if clay is to be had, as follows:

Build a bed of stones, plastering between with clay, $3\frac{1}{2}$ x 4 feet and two feet high. On top of this build a nice rounding pile of dry wood, just the size and shape that the inside of the oven is to be, and fill all of the outside hollows with dry grass or leaves. Now cover this a foot thick with clay, pressing it down firmly to make it into a solid mass. Leave a hole on top at the back end for the smoke to go out and give a draft to the fire when the oven is to be heated. This hole should be about six inches in diameter, and there should be a way of closing it tightly to retain the heat while baking. Leave a larger hole at the front, and also provide a door of some kind. Now let this oven dry about a week, or until you are satisfied that the clay is thoroughly dry. Then set fire to the wood at the opening in front and let it burn out. This will make a good oven for baking bread, biscuits, beans, etc.; also for roasting meats. It should be roofed over to protect it from the storms.

In case there is no clay to be found, a good oven may be made from stones bedded in plaster. The best stones to use are sandstone and slate, as they will stand the fire better than other kinds. For plaster, mix sand, salt and wood

An Outdoor Bake Oven.

ashes. Lime is better than ashes, but cannot be had if one is far from the settlements.

To use this oven, build a good fire in it and keep it going for an hour; then clean out the ashes and embers and place the bread in the oven. Close both openings, and the bread will bake nicely from the heat which is retained by the walls of the oven.

Another very convenient arrangement at the home camp is a cache for keeping fresh meats out of reach of birds, mice, weasels, etc. Four smooth posts should be driven firmly into the ground and allowed to project to a height of four feet. On these lay a platform of poles or split wood. It should be solidly built, for when the meat is frozen one will sometimes want to cut a piece off with the axe. On such a scaffold one can keep all of his game until needed for food. Of course this is only good for northern districts where meats will remain frozen the entire winter. It can be covered with canvas to protect it from the birds.

When camping in a tent and cooking out of doors, there are several little articles, easily made, which help to make cooking easy. For instance, fire tongs. Take a green stick of hardwood about thirty inches long and heat the middle of the stick in the fire; then bend it around a small sapling and tie the ends, leaving it thus until it will remain in a bent shape. The ends can then be flattened, and it will be found useful in picking live coals out of the fire. A fire shovel can be made also out of a piece of tin (an opened tin can), and fixed in the end of a split stick.

CAMERAS AND PHOTOGRAPHY. No outfit is complete without a good camera. With the modern big game hunter the camera is second in im-

portance only to the rifle, and the camper, fisherman and trapper can use one to good advantage.
Photography is interesting, and what can bring
to mind memories of your past pleasant experiences better than a nice collection of photos?
For a number of years past I have carried a camera on the trap line and secured some rare photographs of wild animals, camping scenes, etc.

To the prospective purchaser I will say, buy
the best camera you can afford. Instruction
books are furnished by the manufacturers, and
by following the instructions closely one is certain to get a large per cent of good negatives.
Photography is not as difficult as the amateur
commonly supposes, and any careful person can
learn to operate a camera successfully.

For ordinary use, and especially for hunting,
fishing and the trap line, I advise the use of a
folding film camera. It is true that one can get
a larger per cent. of good photos by using one
of the large plate cameras, but they are heavy
and bulky, and glass plates are not the thing for
the woods. Plate holders must also be loaded in
the dark, and that is inconvenient when in the
woods. If one has a large, bulky camera, he is
likely to leave it at camp too often, and it always
seems that the time when you haven't got the
instrument with you is just the time when it is
most needed.

At present I am using a folding film camera
taking a picture 3¼ x 4¼, and it is a very handy
size, as it folds up into a small package and can
be carried in a large coat pocket or slipped into
the pack. However, if one wishes to get photographs for reproduction, the 4 x 5 size is far better, as five inches is the standard width of the
two-column magazine page. One can sometimes
get a small photo enlarged from the negative,
but a photo for enlargement must be very sharp
and clear, and often a photo which could be
reproduced in exact size would not stand en-
larging.

My camera uses a roll film, consisting of
six or twelve exposures. I use the six exposure
size mostly, as it takes too long to fill out the
double length strip. There are other cameras
using what is called a "film pack," in which the
films lie flat like the pages of a book. These
possess advantages over the roll film, as an exposure can be taken out and developed at any
time without disturbing the remaining ones.

To those who do not understand the prin-
ciples of photography an explanation of the
working of a camera will be of value and will
make my advice more clear. In its simplest
form a camera consists of a box or case in one
end of which is fitted a lens and shutter to admit
the light and reflect the object to be photo-

graphed. In the back is placed the glass plate or celluloid film, which is coated with very sensitive chemicals. These chemicals are affected by the sunlight or artificial light and will when developed show up the scene which was reflected on them when the shutter was open. So sensitive are these films and plates that they would be ruined if exposed to the light for the thousandth part of a second. Glass plates are loaded into plate holders in the dark, and the plate holders may be placed in the camera in any light. Roll films are coiled on a spool, backed by a thick black or red paper, which excludes light, and they may be placed in the camera in daylight. The shutter, which is placed behind the lens, prevents the light from entering and ruining the plate or film, but when one wishes to take a photo he first focuses the camera on the object to be photographed, looking in the view finder, which is simply a small reflecting mirror so arranged that one can see the object as it will appear on the film, and when he has it properly located the operator presses the bulb and springs the shutter. This admits the light, which reflects the view on to the film and makes the impression. The film or plate must then be developed in the dark, and up to this time it must never be exposed to the light for the smallest fraction of a second. The amateur usually lets some professional photographer do the developing, but if he wishes to do it himself it is really much easier than is commonly supposed. After the negative is developed, the photographs are printed on photographic paper by the light of the sun or by artificial light, and the prints must also be developed, each of the photographic papers requiring a different mode of handling. This may also be done by the profess.onal.

The cheapest cameras are only good for snapshots, and they have what is known as a "fixed focus"—that is, they are fairly good for all distances without adjustment; in fact, they cannot be adjusted. The higher priced ones are focussed—that is, the front of the case is drawn out to the proper distance to show the reflection most clearly on the plate. Folding film cameras have a focusing scale graduated for various distances and all that is necessary is for the user to note the distance to the object he wishes to photograph, then draw out the case until the indicator points to that distance on the scale. These cameras are adjustable for snapshots, or, as it is more properly called, instantaneous exposures; also for time exposures. When adjusted for a snapshot, the shutter opens and closes instantly at one pressure of the bulb or lever, and that is the adjustment to use when photographing moving objects, or still objects when the light the light is bright.

A time exposure is a photo taken by exposing the film or plate several seconds, and thus one can get pictures of still objects when the light is too dim for snapshots.

One is just as likely to over-expose the film or plate as to not expose it long enough. This is the difficult part of photography, and the proper time required for exposures can only be learned by experience. When I am doubtful, I make several exposures on different plates, timing each differently. In this way I am more certain to get a good photo.

After a film roll is placed in the camera, one must turn the key until the figure 1 comes under the little window in the back of the case. Then it is ready for taking the first picture. As soon as an exposure is made, turn the key again until the figure 2 is shown, and then it is ready for the second picture. Make this a rule to always turn the key as soon as you have made the exposure, and this will do away with the possibility of taking two pictures on the same film. After all of the films have been exposed, the key is turned and nearly all of the black paper is wound over the film to exclude the light; then the camera is opened and the film, with paper, is strong. One can only take a snapshot when removed for development.

All of the higher grade cameras have shutter stop adjustments, adapting them for various lights. The use of these also must be learned mainly by experience, but the instructions help the beginner.

In taking photos, one must always stand so that the sunlight does not strike on the lens of the camera. A safe rule is to stand with the back to the sun, but if this is not practicable hold one hand so that it shades the lens.

On the whole, photography is decidedly an art, but the beginner, by not trying the more difficult photos and doubtful lights, can get good pictures. It is best for the amateur to confine his work to snapshots and gradually learn time exposures.

Some Advice on Various Subjects. When in camp, always keep the clothing well repaired. Any person going into the woods for some time should carry a repair kit—needles, thread, a few buttons, some patches, scissors, etc. A small rip or tear, if repaired at once, does not make much trouble, but if let go for some time is sure to grow. Such work can be done in the evening and will be a profitable pastime.

Be cleanly about camp. Keep the camp as clean and neat as possible and burn or remove all offal of game and fish from the vicinity. Throw the empty tin cans in the fire and burn them out, as all such refuse serves to attract flies and other vermin in summer.

Here is a good waterproof dressing for leather shoes: Beeswax, tallow and neatsfoot oil, equal parts, heated and mixed. Apply hot. It is good for shoe pacs, and if you are out in the open at any time when the weather is likely or celluloid film, which is coated with very sen- to be wet, use it, and you will find it very good.

When traveling in the fall and early winter, after the ice has formed on the lakes and streams, one is almost certain to walk on the ice whenever possible, even if he knows that it is very dangerous. In such cases always carry a long, slender pole, twenty feet long, if you can get such a one. Grasp it by the middle with both hands and carry it crosswise before you. In case you break through the ice, there will be some hope for you, as the long pole will keep you from going under. Also carry your pack in such a way that it can be easily shaken off in case you do go under.

In winter, in the northern bush never start out for the day without your axe. It is the most indispensable article in the entire outfit. I have gone for a month at a time trapping, without carrying a gun—this in a great game country also—but the axe was always with me. One never knows what may happen to prevent him from returning to camp; and if you must camp out, an hour's work with the axe will enable you to spend the night fairly comfortably, for without a fire it would mean death by freezing. Also keep the ax sharp. A dull ax is of no use in the woods. Never use the ax or knife for digging up the ground. Use the ax to flatten a stout stick and dig with the stick.

In summer always carry some fishing tackle, for, no matter whether the fish are needed badly for food or not, they are always good and are a delightful change from bacon, biscuits and tea. A few hooks and some stout line are all that is necessary. For trout, one can use a scrap of fat bacon to bait the hook, and after one fish is caught a fin or the "throat latch" makes a good bait. If you have no bacon, look for a small frog, a grasshopper or something similar. One can usually find grubs by kicking open an old rotten log, and they make good bait.

In winter, if in the North, carry a few rabbit snares, and whenever possible set them in the evening near the camp. They will provide you with fresh meat and give you bait for the traps.

Always put out the fire before leaving the camp, and when you go outside take a good look at the roof, if it is dry. This I learned from experience to be a good rule, for at one time I

was careless, and the result was that on my return one evening I found my camp and outfit a
pile of smoking embers.

In the woods, always be careful about fire.
Never light your pipe and drop the match in the
dry leaves; and be careful that you do not empty
your pipe in a place where it could possibly start
a forest fire.   Be equally careful when building
fires for camping purposes.   A forest fire may
not only destroy your camp, but it may ruin
your hunting grounds also and destroy property
for other persons, if near the settlement.   I have
spent the greater portion of my life in the woods,
one place and another, and never yet started a
forest fire.

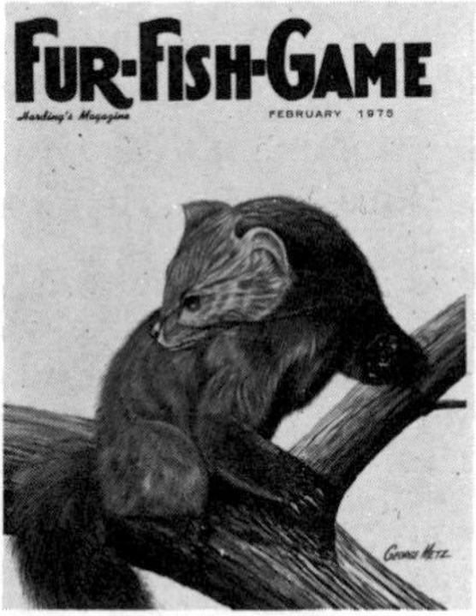
FUR-FISH-GAME
Harding's Magazine
FEBRUARY 1975
George Metz